Many churches put young people and adults in different boxes, because it just seems so hard to cater for them together. Jason offers a vision of an intergenerational church where people of all ages worship together, learning with and from each other. This excellent book is full of cultural analysis, practical advice and wisdom for a way forward. You need to read it.
Jenny Baker, writer and founder of the Sophia Network for women in youth work.

In *Mend the Gap* Jason Gardner has given us not only a theological and cultural critique of the church's relationship with young people, but real world strategies for putting it right. Youth leaders will find inspiration and encouragement for their ministry here, but really this should be in the hands of every church leader too. If there was ever a time to think about the gap it's now, and this book ignites the debate that should be taking place in every church.
Chris Curtis, Director, The Luton Churches Education Trust

Some of greatest kingdom advances happen when someone steps out of the trenches for a few moments and surveys the battlefield. Could it be that we're all scurrying in a certain direction due to the dangerous mix of desperation and tradition? Could it be that we're playing our part in fracturing the family of God through our desire for numerical gain and the comfort of segregation? This book is a challenge to all of us to be tellers of the story not simply where it's easy, within our own generation, but also where some translation will be necessary, both up and down the generations, forging family ties that will last.
Andy Flannagan, author and singer-songwriter

The whole force of western culture is to divide the generations. This book takes on the absolutely vital task of bringing the generations back together again, and does so with cultural insight,

biblical rigour, love for young people and confidence in the potential of the local church.
Mark Greene, London Institute for Contemporary Christianity

Mend the Gap is a refreshing blend of readable cultural analysis, thought provoking reflection and practical suggestions. Born out of a deep concern, yet brimming with optimism the pages of this book contain a wake up call. Read it and act!
*Phil Green, Evangelical Alliance – *__essential__ project*

This book highlights fresh thinking to show working with young people should be for all. Every member of every church should read this book!
Katy Johnson, Youthworker

I have seen Jason brilliantly bridge the generation gap in his local church and now he brings his grassroots experience together with some critical thinking to produce an urgently needed book that will benefit the whole church.
Dr Krish Kandiah, Executive Director, Churches in Mission Evangelical Alliance UK

Jason Gardner has produced a compelling insight into the challenges of creating and cherishing multi-generational church. With a detailed and astute analysis of the history of adolescence and youth culture, and the journey of the church alongside these phenomena, this book finishes by providing those involved in youth ministry with some realistic and wonderfully counter-cultural ideas for ensuring the Church becomes a place where those of all ages can interact and grow as followers of Christ.
Jill Rowe, Oasis UK Church & Community Development Director

Discipleship is a word banded around by many people working with young people these days – sadly many people do not know what it means to think about and practice discipleship. Want to know more about discipling young people and mending the gap between generations? Read this book.
Tim Sudworth, Youth Pastor and author of Mission-Shaped Youth

I couldn't put this book down – not just because it's so well researched, written and thought through – but because it dares to prophetically and powerfully challenge the compartmentalizing of church whilst offering some practical suggestions on how to build a vibrant cross-generational community. This book isn't just for youth leaders and church leaders – it's for all of us!
Matt Summerfield, Executive Director, Urban Saints

MEND THE GAP

MEND THE GAP

CAN THE CHURCH RECONNECT THE GENERATIONS?

Jason Gardner

ivp

Inter-Varsity Press
Norton Street, Nottingham NG7 3HR, England
Email: ivp@ivpbooks.com
Website: www.ivpbooks.com

First published 2008

British Library Cataloguing in Publication Data
A catalogue record for this book is available from the British Library.

UK ISBN: 978-1-84474-284-4

Set in Monotype Dante 12/15pt
Typeset in Great Britain by CRB Associates, Reepham, Norfolk
Printed and bound in Great Britain by Ashford Colour Press Ltd, Gosport, Hampshire

Inter-Varsity Press publishes Christian books that are true to the Bible and that communicate the gospel, develop discipleship and strengthen the church for its mission in the world.

Inter-Varsity Press is closely linked with the Universities and Colleges Christian Fellowship, a student movement connecting Christian Unions in universities and colleges throughout Great Britain, and a member movement of the International Fellowship of Evangelical Students. Website: *www.uccf.org.uk*

CONTENTS

INTRODUCTION

> I would that there were no age between sixteen and three and twenty, or that youth would sleep out the rest; for there is nothing in the between but getting wenches with child, wronging the ancientry, stealing, fighting.
> (Shakespeare, *The Winter's Tale*)

We were all young once. We all have our tales of playful – or serious – rebellion against the restraints placed upon us by our elders. We all reminisce over the pop music loves of our era, insisting that 'those were the days when music was music – not like today'. In turn Elvis, Bowie, Bono, Cobain or Eminem usurped the throne as 'King of Pop' and, in turn, became the thorn in the side of parents' sensibilities.

In many ways the conflict between young and old seems to be a repetitive cycle: generations of parents will visit upon their offspring the battles they fought with their own parents – over the hemline of a skirt, front door lockdown time, favourable or unfavourable peer affiliations, TV, film and now internet censorship. As any parent knows, the list is endless.

But is it fair to envisage the gap between youth and adult cultures as a battle? And if so, is it true that such a fight has always existed, or has it only escalated into a full-scale 'war' within the space of the last century?

Many believe the latter. Yes, youth has always had a voice distinct from that of its elders, but events of the twentieth century led to that voice growing in presence, volume and stark contrast to the opinions expressed by the mainstream 'norm'.

In our lifetime, we've witnessed the birth of a new phenomenon in terms of world history – the emergence of youth culture. It's a collective story whose narrative is defined by its very opposition to adult culture.

The rise and rise of youth culture through the latter half of the twentieth century led to an inevitable distancing between generations – the proverbial generation gap. It has led to splits in families. It has often divided whole nations in opposing political stances and differing definitions of what constitutes the moral consensus – as the 'radical' 1960s demonstrated.

The gap between generations is nowhere better illustrated than within the church. This is mainly because the church as a family is dedicated to keeping that family whole: our mission statement is to unite people across divisions of race, opinion, sex and age.

This is, to an extent, at variance with the current climate. A consumer-based society is content to let people create their own self-serving communities that allow individuals as much freedom as possible – the 'atomization' of society. It has little objection to social groupings that are based around peers or interest groups rather than families – a trend that's currently growing and one that, at least in part, was spawned by the birth of youth culture.

The church, however, has a commitment to 'family values' and to keeping a sense of unity amongst its diverse members. So it feels keenly the departure of so many young people from its midst. Recent figures show that around 1,000 young people currently leave the church every week.

Such a 'divorce' only serves to highlight the generational differences between sectors of the church. There have been a number of church splits, or perhaps a better expression is church evolutions, in response to the issue. Splits have often traditionally occurred over disputes about doctrine. These latest divides, however, have occurred as a result of churches no longer addressing the needs of burgeoning generations.

We've witnessed the development of alternative worship communities, emerging churches, youth churches and youth congregations, all relatively new forms of church that appeal to distinct generations.

Most churches are genuinely concerned about protecting the diversity of God's family and that means including all ages at all costs. But the endless adverts for youth workers in Christian publications indicate that the church is extremely concerned with securing a future for itself – as well it should be. At the moment the church at large suffers from having an alarming deficit of young people. Over the course of the 1990s, some 500,000 children stopped going to church.[1]

It may come as no surprise, then, that the church employs more youth workers than any other institution including the government. It's also no surprise that because of the high expectations placed upon the role, many youth workers become disillusioned or the victims of burnout. The need to reach young people is so great that many youth leaders are often expected to be sowers, reapers and keepers.

We have to realize that the problems highlighted by generational differences are really evidence of teething troubles. The difficulties faced within church and society are the direct result of an acceleration in cultural change that no one in the church could have predicted or been prepared for.

The cultural landscape of Britain has obviously changed drastically over the last hundred years. Technological advance and the growth in affluence in the West have been the main drivers of this transformation – factors that we'll explore later. Some have dealt with these changes. Some have sought to ignore them. Those born into them have become used to the ground moving beneath their feet and so simply adapt to each new phase in culture.

This is, of course, old news. But the church still has to grasp that it is seeking to marry together social groupings with widely diverse views and that to a large extent its attempts are failing.

BBC Radio 4 recently provided an excellent example of just how much society has changed. The programme focused on the culture clashes experienced by individuals who had only recently taken up residency in the UK. A Ghanaian father of four remarked on the reluctance of Britons to bring up other people's children. He was referring to the lack of a communal sense of parenting and cited an instance when he chided a group of young boys who were throwing stones at a building. Their response to his attempts at discipline was a barrage of insults.

This would not have happened in Ghana, he said. This would not have happened in Britain – forty or fifty years ago. The boys would have grown up honouring the requests of elders inside and outside the home, even if those requests were made by strangers. Old age alone would have commanded respect. Times have changed. The world of Western Europeans and the world of those within developing countries seem worlds apart, although, as globalization accelerates, those worlds are growing ever closer.

It's a point that church historian Meic Pearse made in a lecture series at the London Institute for Contemporary Christianity (LICC) entitled 'Why the Rest Hates the West'. One of the reasons why non-Western countries take issue with the West is the changing attitudes to the family. For non-Western societies, strong family units are seen as perhaps the essential ingredient of a 'civilized' country. Conversely, the breakdown of the family within the Western hemisphere is seen as the cost of becoming 'civilized'. This perhaps says more about our adherence to capitalism and consumerism than it does about our understanding of what it means to be truly 'civil' to one another.

And you don't need to have arrived in Britain from another country to experience culture shock. For many adults it occurs when they accidentally switch on to MTV or visit the church youth group.

If we're going to seek to answer the question, 'Can the schism between young and old ever be bridged?' we will first have to examine more thoroughly the relevant cultural revolutions of the twentieth century. In the chapters ahead we'll see what part they've played in creating the gap, whilst also looking at the implications for the church, before moving on to how the church should be and is responding. But first, one key to understanding the generation gap is to see just how radical the cultural changes of the twentieth century have been.

Stark change creates static

In the twelfth century the wise old sage Peter the Hermit remarked, 'Youth has no regard for old age and the wisdom of the centuries is looked down upon both as stupid and foolishness.'[2] That verdict has echoed *ad nauseam* throughout the centuries. It appears that the old have often looked down on the culture of young people with a certain amount of trepidation, if not outright disdain.

The problem is, though, that it's not simply differences in generational cultures that can cause apoplexy: it's the rate at which cultural change now takes place. It's like a 1920s Model T Ford being outstripped by a Ferrari at the traffic lights – the Ford driver hasn't the ability or desire to catch up with the Ferrari and is probably slightly outraged at any suggestion that he should want to travel at such a blistering pace.

There is resistance to change precisely because cultural shift has accelerated, creating too much of a distance between generations for the older generation to catch up. If we could have spread the technological advances of the latter twentieth century over a millennium, things might have been different. People generally find it easier to adapt to more gradual change. Society moved so fast, however, and the difference between generations seemed so marked, that the older generation found the change hard to comprehend or approve of. They were therefore reluctant to move with the times.

Stark change has created static – something unmoving and passive. Often, when we're trying to implement change in the church, we come up against seemingly immovable forces that create 'generational tension'.

It's easy to understand why this became the case. Imagine having grown up in a Britain united in solidarity through the war, only to face the cultural upheaval of the late 1950s and 60s: the increasing immigration of ethnic minorities into the UK; the impact of TV, radio and film on family life; the subsequent creation of the film and rock'n'roll superstar thanks to global TV; the rapid growth in drug culture thanks to Swiss scientist Albert Hoffman's accidental discovery of LSD; the end of national service in 1960 which ushered in a new sense of freedom for young men, who no longer had to fear a stint in the military; the initiation of the sexual revolution and the advance of feminism, largely thanks to the creation of the Pill. These changes effectively placed a jemmy between the generations, prising them apart and creating distinct cultural identities. The difference between young people in the late 1950s and early 60s and preceding generations was as distinct as the contrast between black-and-white and colour TV, as the following quote from Paul McCartney demonstrates.

In response to the question, 'Were you a hellraiser?' McCartney replied, 'In terms of girls? Not unlike any other young guy at the time. The Pill had just come in. That was a very handy thing. Suddenly women were prepared to sleep with a fellah with no great risk of pregnancy. Now we could all have some fun. Everyone started looking sharper, had a little bit of money in their pockets, there were clubs to go to, good music to listen to . . . it was like a paradise had been created for young people – a time when everything was switched on at once. There were all these possibilities opening up that our parents could only have dreamed about. Suddenly, our entire world was bright colours.'[3]

In the light of such cultural revolutions, it's not surprising that the maintenance of tradition and certain customs became requisite for an older generation in order to provide them with an anchor in the midst of such uncertainty. Is it any wonder, then, that older members of our churches may prove indignant when the church insists on changing with the times?

This cultural upheaval has often resulted in a conflict of expectation in churches – whether it's over questions of mission to today's generations or service style. But is aggravation between differing generations of Christians inevitable? We have to figure out whether this unique point in church history will result in a parting of the ways or a uniting across age barriers. While successive generations live next door to each other geographically, culturally they seem to be in two very different worlds. The church is in a special position in that it's one of the few sections of society that's still actively trying to bring the two worlds together. Unfortunately this often happens in the form of a collision rather than the creation of a harmonious whole.

It's the new wine for new wineskins dilemma, if you like. Do we need to accept that in many places the church simply needs to rip it up and start again, to prune savagely in order to create new growth? Are the generations born into the post-World War II communications explosion more likely to be able to adapt to quick changes in culture? And if so, will they be the ones to take the church forward in an ever-changing world, while the generations who are used to slower cultural change will inevitably resist the quick-change culture and eventually peter out?

We can see where this is happening in Britain. The church is experiencing segregation: we do have instances where young people are being drained from existing churches into youth churches or youth congregations. And many pastors or youth workers can testify to the strain of seeking to forge change in churches where change is often simply not wanted.

The conflict between the expectations of young and old for church services is just one example of this. When young people 'do' church, it turns out very different from adult church. The organ is replaced with DJ equipment, the lighting becomes less Methodist and more Ministry of Sound, and so on. Many churches often allow such services to take place only once a month. This provides a separate space for young people rather than seeking to blend in elements they'll appreciate in every Sunday service. As such, it's a fairly ineffectual placebo aimed at young people. This is where the generation gap becomes evident, and this book is dedicated to looking at how deep the problem is in the church and gauging whether our efforts so far have been successful, simply adequate, or plain misguided.

In order to do this, we'll have to map out our territory. The first chapter of the book deals with a bit of history – tracing social changes at the beginning of the twentieth century that had huge consequences for the creation of youth culture.

Chapters 2, 3 and 4 concentrate on factors that added to the growth of youth culture and help to sustain it. We'll be dealing with consumerism and globalization, the rise of peer pressure and the huge role that information and communications technology has played in aiding the divide between young and old.

Chapter 5 aims to outline a serious by-product of twentieth- and twenty-first-century life: the blurring of boundaries between childhood and adulthood and how this impacts the way we do youth work.

In response, chapter 6 takes a look at how the Bible views the differing roles of adults and children and how we can take its cue when it comes to passing on faith.

Chapters 7 and 8 deal with the church's response to the generation gap and suggest that the church needs to reassess seriously its mission to young people and how we meet, worship and teach as God's kingdom on earth.

Chapter 9 sets out some ways forward, suggesting possible solutions to bridging the gap, detailing examples of pioneers in this area and outlining important lessons that the church in today's world needs to take on board.

In conclusion, chapter 10 proposes an answer to the question at hand: can intergenerational church succeed?

Throughout I'll reflect on how today's culture has shaped the way we reach and teach young people, and how the church needs to take the reins back and lead culture in the way we treat our young people.

It's at this point, as a member of Generation X (roughly those born between 1965 and 1980) who understands the wants of that particular cultural 'brand', that I hesitantly suggest that this book is more of a dialogue than a series of answers. I hesitate on two accounts. First, because many people would simply prefer a good old 'how to make your church an intergenerational success' and they might stop reading now (perhaps another example of 'generational tension'). Second, because it obviously isn't simply a dialogue. I hope it's something of a wake-up call. I hope it's incisive enough for churches all over Britain to make serious changes to the way they practise. And I hope it's not over-ambitious and too far reaching in the way it attempts to accomplish this.

So read on. At the end you may want to fire your youth worker or hire four more. You may decide to shift your church into a neo-hippie eco-friendly commune, or you may simply want to add more smells and a few new bells. You may want to chuck out your TV and your PC, or you may want to run workshops for eight-year-olds on debugging the latest version of Windows. But what I really hope you take away from this book is that Christ's ability to inspire a whole big bad beautiful mix of people to follow him, regardless of their age, has not diminished, but burns more brightly and more strongly than it did 2,000 years ago.

Notes

1. P. Brierley, *Pulling Out of the Nosedive*, pp. 111–113.
2. D. Hilborn and M. Bird (eds), *God and the Generations*, p. 3.
3. Taken from an interview in *Uncut* magazine, July 2004.

PART 1

MAKING THE GAP: YOUTH CULTURE AND CONSUMPTION

1. IN THE BEGINNING: EMPIRE IDEALS AND ADOLESCENCE

> I see no hope for the future of our people if they are dependent on the frivolous youth of today, for certainly all youth are reckless beyond words. When I was a boy, we were taught to be discreet and respectful of elders, but the present youth are exceedingly unwise and impatient of restraint.
> (Hesiod, Greek poet, 700 BC)

> . . . without some ability to understand youth's existence as a social relation, the complex forces that give form and content to the lives of the young become impossible to comprehend.
> (Phil Mizen, *The Changing State of Youth*)[1]

As Hesiod's quote highlights, the old have often despaired of the young on the grounds that the future of society rests on their shoulders. Although such concerns have been aired throughout history, they came to a crescendo at the beginning of the twentieth century. Thanks to the fruits of industrialization, European empires had expanded all over the globe. As Britain would find out, however, the maintenance of those empires depended entirely upon the state of the nation's youth.

So the second quote is an apology for this first chapter's headlong dive into history. Much of contemporary society's approach to young people is rooted in the social 'earthquakes' of the late nineteenth and early twentieth centuries. In order to understand how we relate to young people today, we have to delve into the cultural traditions and attitudes surrounding 'youth' that have sprung up over the past 150 years or so.

Fake expectations?

As the number of prime-time TV hours dedicated to 'improving' our teens increases (*Brat Camp*, Ian Wright's *Unfit Kids*, etc.), it serves only to remind us that we believe society's success lies in how our culture influences and forms our young. Writer Lev Grossman states, 'When it comes to social change, pop culture is the most sensitive of seismometers.'[2] The media's fascination with troubled youth tells us that there's a huge concern over the state of young people. If we fail them, we fail ourselves – and TV seems to be suggesting that we're doing precisely that.

When it comes to looking at the prospects of society, or discussing the moral health of the nation, the debate frequently focuses on the current condition of youth culture. As psychologist Christine Griffin notes,

> Young people are assumed to hold the key to the nation's future, and the treatment and management of youth is expected to provide the solution to a nation's problems from drug abuse, hooliganism and teenage pregnancy to inner city riots.[3]

Such attitudes are prevalent in society and they do underline the heavy expectations that are placed on our youth. At one time, when notions of citizenship had not been superseded by consumerist ideals, it was seen as the responsibility of the community at large as well as the state to nurture positive ambitions within the young and also to develop an understanding of social responsibility.

However, in today's society the adult populace is reluctant to commit much spare time to providing a space where young people may be educated about their role in society, or can at least establish healthy mentor relationships with adults (both the Girl Guides and Scouts associations, for example, are currently desperately short of volunteers).[4] Often the only people providing such a role are youth work professionals or teachers via the citizenship curriculum. There's a certain hypocrisy in maintaining high expectations for our young whilst rarely lifting a finger to contribute to the fostering of such ideals ourselves.

Nonetheless, as a brief review of the history of the late nineteenth and early twentieth centuries suggests, it was the extreme pressure placed upon young people to live up to social ideals – to create a flourishing and morally upright society (and, of course, to maintain 'progress') – that actually led to divisions between young and old. This current obsession with the *state of young people today* is one we've inherited.

Empire ideals

At the dawn of the twentieth century, the South African war raised concerns over the poor performance of young British soldiers.[5] As the structure of the Empire depended on its ability to police and extend its borders through military might, Britain became obsessed with how best it might improve the mental and physical health of its young men.

The young were seen as the formational blocks of a healthy society. As Nancy Lesko notes in *Act Your Age*, her treatise on adolescence in the twentieth century, a 'strong fear of decline [is] a central component of the discourse of civilization and its technologies of progress'.[6] Question: How do we stop the rot? Answer: Through the rigorous education of the young. Hence the public school system excelled in taking young white males and placing them in a strict regime of mental and physical education, in order to rob them of the wayward and distracting emotions and motivations of adolescence. (The schools were single sex to remove boys from the 'feminizing' effects of women.) Robert Baden-Powell, an army general and hero of the South African war, provided his solution to the 'youth problem' in the form of the Boy Scouts – a regime of healthy outdoor activity and community service that encouraged within its members loyalty towards adults and Empire.

Of course, the emphasis was on producing 'sociable' European white men, as they would be the mainstay of any successful empire. Darwin's theories of evolution had been bastardized and subsumed under the rhetoric of the pompous Empire machine. 'Survival of the fittest' was key, and as white European males dominated the globe, it was obvious that they were at the top of the pyramid, arch-predators in the scheme of life. Inspired by Darwin, social theorists and scientists drew up a pecking order for Homo sapiens:

> The Great Chain of Being; a rank ordering of species from the least primitive to the most civilized, based on evolutionary theory. The great chain of being located white European men and their societies' norms and values at the pinnacle of civilization and morality.[7]

They largely saw the natives of colonized nations as primitives, forming the lower ranks of the 'Chain of Being', in need of education, civilization and discipline in order for them to advance. The young white male was seen in the same light, as Alan Prout and Allison James point out:

> During the 19th century western sociological theorists, the self-elected representatives of rationality, saw in other cultures primitive forms of the human condition. These they

> regarded as childish in their simplicity and irrational in their belief . . . the savage was seen as the precursor of civilized man paralleling the way that the child prefigured adult life.[8]

It's easy to trace the current 'moral panics' over the state of our youth today back to these earlier paranoias about the future of the Empire and the need to control and coerce the young in order for them to become 'good citizens'. We can also trace back to this age the development of the idea that institutions, not families or communities, took the dominant role in nurturing responsibility within the young. This was obviously reflected in the various Christian-based youth organizations that sprang up during this period – for example, Sunday schools, Crusaders, Boys' Brigade and Campaigners.

The fact that many parents today blame 'school' for their children's behaviour may be partly due to the influence of consumerism, but it is also due to the influence of this dependency on institutions. For instance, the daily papers recently reported that some parents were insisting that the school should decide when their children were to go to bed.

It's a question to which we'll be returning: have families within the church become too dependent on the institution of youth work to raise their children within the faith community?

Education, adolescence and more expectations

Once upon a time, the move from child to adult was relatively easily marked. As Christine Griffin remarks,

> In pre-industrial European societies there was no clear distinction between childhood and other pre-adult phases of

> life. The main stages of childhood, youth and adulthood were defined primarily in relation to one's degree of dependence or separation from the family of origin.[9]

Adulthood was defined by economic 'emancipation' – the ability to support yourself (or contribute to the support of the family) via work or by getting married during your early teen years. There existed no limbo period during which children had time to evolve emotionally as well as physically into 'grown ups'.

One of the main impacts of the industrial advances of the late nineteenth century that contributed to the evolution of youth culture was the creation of greater wealth for society as a whole and more disposable incomes for families – the expansion of the middle classes. Children were no longer expected to support themselves with full-time work. More and more families could also afford to put their children through further education. It was no longer the preserve of the elite.

The role of education in creating strong bonds amongst peer groups cannot be underestimated. In 1875 the US government set aside tax monies to provide further tutelage for American children, extending education from the age of 14 to 17. Other countries followed suit. In Britain in 1880 school attendance for 5- to 10-year-olds became compulsory, and by 1918 the school leaving age was 14.[10]

Lengthening the period young people spent more or less exclusively among their peer group had obvious ramifications for the development of youth culture. In the late 1950s only 4% of the UK population was in higher education. Today, with more and more people heading into further education (the British government has approved a target to see 50% of young people in tertiary education), the crucial role that higher education has played in cementing peer group affiliations is immeasurable.

For many young people at university, their early adult years are lived within the context of independence from parental influence and the freedom of celebrating being 18-plus amongst their peers. As a result, many young people's first experience of adulthood is one that is largely detached from any sense of social responsibility. The main commitment is, of course, to study for a degree, but the lifestyle that often accompanies it becomes the basis for people's experience of 'adult' life – good times with friends.

Another area of nineteenth-century progress that certainly helped sow the seeds of twentieth-century youth culture was the development of the social sciences, in particular psychology and its re-evaluation of childhood development. So a crucial factor in the creation of the teenager was a switch in definitions: 'adulthood' was no longer arrived at through economic independence, but through a biological journey that came to be termed 'adolescence' – 'the period of rapid growth that occurs between childhood and adulthood'.[11] It's a word derived from old French via Latin that simply means 'grow up' (ironically a frequent instruction aimed at teenagers by their parents).

It was American psychologist G. Stanley Hall who instigated this change in perception and coined the phrase. He focused on the onset of puberty as the defining shift away from childhood. This meant that the main emphasis in the understanding of this transition period was on the biological aspect of 'growing up', centring on physiological drives that led to 'sexual awakening'.[12]

Hall referred to the 'hormonal upheaval' undergone during 'adolescence' as the 'storm and stress' period when young people experienced conflicts related to sexuality and self-identity. It was seen as a time where the 'freedom' of youth needed to be tempered with a healthy amount of discipline in order to control 'unhelpful' impulses, particularly of a sexual nature.[13] Hall's 'storm and stress' theory is without doubt the birthing ground of the myth of the 'troubled teens', a time when young people are inevitably set apart from the 'normal' world of adults.

As Bradford Brown and Larson note, this view of adolescence became prevalent particularly in the US and in Britain:

> The common term for adolescence in the United States, *teenager*, brings forth images of recklessness, rebellion, irresponsibility, and conflict – hardly a flattering portrait but one that captures the worried stance that most adults in society take towards young people.[14]

So adolescence came to be seen as a 'cocoon' period from which would emerge the adult of the species. It was thought that exerting a certain influence on the environment of the young during this period of identity searching would result in the 'moulding' of an ideal adult. This is illustrated, as mentioned previously, by the harsh upbringing boys had within the public school system.

Allowing uncertainties over the 'maintenance' of progress and the stability and future of the nation to impact society's perception and treatment of the young had major repercussions. One such development was the 'commodification' of youth. Producing healthy and intellectual adults with an appetite for competition who were also responsible citizens would obviously have positive implications for the future of industry. This was a notion still alive and kicking in the late twentieth century, as highlighted by this quote from John Akers, chairman of IBM in the 1980s:

> Education isn't just a social concern, it's a major economic concern. If our students can't compete today, how will our companies compete tomorrow?[15]

Lesko concludes that educational policy is largely governed by a desire to protect industry and commerce and encourage notions of social equilibrium – and so, to an extent, schooling seeks to manipulate young people into becoming 'productive' members of society.[16] As she points out, teenagers are 'carefully attuned to adults' overt and covert messages'. The adult populace's obsession with young people creating an economically viable future for themselves, as primarily 'producers' within society ('What do you want to do when you grow up?'), thus becomes a source of tension and can lead to alienation.

Society sends out mixed messages, particularly when it comes to ideas of what constitutes success. Popular culture, of infinite importance to the young, dictates that the future holds wealth and fame. As Christopher Lasch notes, 'Success in our society has to be ratified by publicity.'[17] A recent survey amongst 14-year-old girls asked what they wanted to be by the time they were 21. The answers were 'rich', 'famous' and 'married' – they wanted to be Posh Spice. Their education, on the other hand, seeks to prepare them only for a role in the 'real world', which is, of course, within the interminable world of work: a clash, then, of ideals and expectations.

Another emphasis of the explosion of social sciences and the turn-of-the-century debates over the governance of youth was the deliberate desire to delay adulthood. Through better diets and healthcare, the physical attributes of adult growth, such as the menarche, were occurring earlier.[18] It has already been noted that the young were compared to 'primitives' in terms of their mental and physical capabilities. In order for them to become fully integrated members of society, it was thought proper to defend against precocity (early development) and to do so by extending the period in which they were economically dependent on adults so that they could 'mature' properly.

Encouraging young people to stay on in higher education was one way to accomplish this. It also extended the period in which they came directly under the scrutiny of adults and institutions. Adolescents were largely treated as children. They were not granted responsible roles, as it was feared this would bring about independence and premature 'adulthood'. So, for example, around the turn of the century, many adolescents who had been Sunday school teachers were demoted to 'being merely pupils'.[19] And, of course, up until the late 1800s children had been part of the world of work, which placed them directly alongside adults. As Caroline Chartres comments, 'Even in the affluent west children were an essential part of the workforce until the 19th century.'[20] The Bill making it illegal to employ anyone under 10 was only passed in 1876.

Yet another concern for those who sought to advance society at the turn of the century (and still today in the twenty-first century) was what young people did with their spare time. It was deemed that a child with too much time on its hands might indeed turn to the devil's work. Hence the drive to keep children in further education and the setting up of extracurricular programmes such as the Scouts and Girl Guides (the girls were to be 'Guides', not 'Scouts', because they were to seek to become 'better mothers and "guides" to the next generation'[21]).

It's easy to see how all these factors contribute to the discourse on youth and powerlessness. Young people were no longer entrusted with responsibility, their role in education was mainly passive, they were endlessly supervised and 'nannied' inside and outside school, all as part of society's desire to progress. They were 'human beings in progress', uniformly regarded as being part of a 'transitional' stage; they had not yet 'become' anything, they were only 'becoming'. As such, their role in society had been reduced from that of active participants in the world of work to that of passive templates on which the hierarchies at large would imprint their hopes and fears for the future of society.

It's fitting to end this section with an incisive summary by Lesko of Allison James and Alan Prout, of the dependency that has been engendered in young people by a century's imposition of exacting expectations. The language of development and evolution has come to dominate our perceptions of youth and influence the need to control their environment. It's no wonder, then, that young people may feel, to a degree, suspended or 'lost' in time,[22] and our attempts to nurture maturity have actually resulted in the opposite.

> Teenagers cannot go backward to childhood nor forward to adulthood 'before their time' without incurring derogatory labels, for example 'immature,' 'loose,' or 'precocious.' The dominant concepts regarding youth's position in the western societies, 'development' and 'socialization,' make it impossible for youth to exercise power over life events or to represent themselves, since they are not fully developed or socialized.[23]

Conclusion

Youth culture's roots can be traced to particular driving forces within the rapidly changing world of politics, industry and society at large within the latter part of the nineteenth century and the twentieth century. Also, a concept central to our cultural understanding of youth, 'adolescence', is a relatively recent phenomenon.[24] These social forces helped blur the boundaries between childhood and adulthood and encouraged society's obsession with the nannying of youth. In effect it stopped the transition from child to adult being an 'organic', undisputed, community affair and turned it into something that was managed by the state.

Such blurring of definitions has led to continued social uncertainty over how we view children, something we'll focus on in chapter 5. But for now it's safe to say that recently we've lost confidence when it comes to *knowing* how to treat children – we're unsure whether we should fear them or protect them. This is as true in the church as it is in society as a whole. As David Buckingham points out,

> On the one hand children are increasingly seen as threatened and endangered. Thus we have seen a succession of high profile investigations into child abuse, both in families and in schools and children's homes . . . On the other hand, children are also increasingly perceived as a threat to us – as violent, anti-social and sexually precocious. There has been growing concern about the apparent collapse of discipline in schools, and the rise in child crime, drug-taking and teenage pregnancy.[25]

The acceleration of industry and the inception of adolescence were just the birthing ground for confusion over the place of children in society. Soon to add to that mix was the post-war boom in consumerism.

Notes

1. P. Mizen, *The Changing State of Youth*, p. 5.
2. L. Grossman, 'Grow up? Not so fast', *Time Magazine*, 2005.

3. C. Griffin, 'Representations of the Young', in J. Roche and S. Tucker (eds), *Youth in Society*, p. 17.
4. A. Sieghart, 'The Bill that will kill trust between the generations', *The Times*, 2006.
5. S. Rogers, 'Making and Moulding of Modern Youth', in Roche and Tucker, *Youth in Society*, p. 10.
6. N. Lesko, *Act Your Age*, p. 26.
7. Ibid., p. 20.
8. Ibid., pp. 22–26.
9. Griffin, 'Representations of the Young', p. 18.
10. Statistics from Department for Education and Skills, www.dfes.gov.uk.
11. E. Atwater, *Adolescence*, p. 4.
12. C. Griffin, *Representations of Youth*, p. 15.
13. Griffin, 'Representations of the Young', p. 19.
14. B. Bradford Brown and R. W. Larson, 'The Kaleidoscope of Adolescence', in B. Bradford Brown *et al.* (eds), *The World's Youth*, p. 6.
15. Lesko, *Act Your Age*, p. 96.
16. Ibid., pp. 96–97.
17. G. Cray, 'Reaching for the Stars', *Third Way*, 2000.
18. J. C. Coleman and L. B. Hendry, *The Nature of Adolescence*, pp. 30–32.
19. Lesko, *Act Your Age*, p. 63.
20. K. White and C. Chartres, 'State of Grace', *Third Way*, 2002.
21. Lesko, *Act Your Age*, p. 80.
22. A. James and A. Prout, 'Re-Presenting Childhood: Time and Transition in the Study of Childhood', in A. James and A. Prout (eds), *Constructing and Reconstructing Childhood*, pp. 233–234.
23. Lesko, *Act Your Age*, p. 123.
24. R. Frankel, *The Adolescent Psyche*, pp. 4–5.
25. D. Buckingham, *After the Death of Childhood*, p. 3.

2. THE COST OF COOL: THE IMPACT OF CONSUMERISM

> Everyone's a teenager now . . .
> (Robert Elms, writer and broadcaster)

It will come as no surprise to any parent used to balancing budgets to allow for Nintendo, Nike and Nokia that consumer pressure plays a big part in the life of the twenty-first-century boy or girl. The price tag placed on seeing a child through the first 18 years of life on earth is apparently £140,000. As one newspaper recently contested, you could buy a house for that, or, if you live in London, at least a well-decorated garage. Today the average child's bedroom is likely to contain £1,500 worth of gadgets and toys.[1]

We're well aware of the increasing cost of bringing up children. We're also aware of the pressures placed on parents who both have to find work in order to finance the rising costs of family living. We're also more than a little alarmed by the emerging phenomena of KGOY – Kids Growing Older Younger. We've seen the birth of the 'tweenagers', 8- and 9-year-olds who have acquired the spending habits of teenagers, hankering after mobile phones, fashion accessories and music to boot. And we're justifiably disturbed by the often casual adoption of a sexuality that belies children's pre-pubescent years –sexually charged fashions encouraged by a swathe of pop-culture role models aimed at pre-teen audiences. It's currently a growing trend. The modern adolescent girl will see more stylish and sexualized images of the female form in one day than her mother's generation would have seen throughout their entire teenage years.

However, the media's constant portrayal of the perfect youthful image as the ultimate in desirability has also resulted in a reverse of the trend mentioned above: teenagers may want to be adults, but also, as Robert Elms inferred, adults now want to be teenagers. Instead of it being simply Kids Growing Older Younger, we also have ASYO – Adults Staying Younger Older. Mothers and daughters shop at the same stores. Late twenty-something and early thirty-something males (the 'kidult' phenomenon) still play video games (only now they refer to their toys as 'gadgets'), and 2.3 million cosmetic surgery procedures a year in the UK indicate that the fountain of youth is squarely located in Harley Street.

We may be heading towards the blandest period in consumer history when everyone from the age of 8 to 80 looks the same, dresses the same and everybody listens to Robbie Williams.

The branding of youth

In *Cool Rules*, Pountain and Robins define 'cool' as

> an attitude or personality type that has emerged in many different societies, during different historical epochs, and which has served different social functions, but is nevertheless recognizable as a particular combination of three core personality traits, namely narcissism, ironic detachment and hedonism.[2]

It's an accurate description, and those three ingredients have been effectively bottled and served up in anything from adverts through to punk bands and via big-screen anti-hero youth icons.

Being 'cool' is what youth culture is all about, and the marketing of 'cool' has ensured that youth culture is the most successful brand on the market – a brand that is forever expanding. As one commentator put it, 'The trouble with "teenage" is that it has been appropriated by everyone and sold back so often that the appropriation is all we recognise now.'[3]

It's so exponential that although we used to think of 'youth culture' as referring to those in their early to late teens, we now also associate it with pre- and post-teen groups. So monikers such as 'tweenager', 'kidult', 'Gen X' or 'Gen Y' are often simply used to describe slightly variant groups within the umbrella target market that is youth culture.

This isn't a new fad, though. The term 'teenager' itself, coined in the early 1950s by advertisers, was used in exactly the same way – to identify a newly emergent group of young people with spending power. This group were adolescents who had their own disposable income thanks to the post-war economic boom. It inevitably led to a tailored market being produced for youth, of which rock'n'roll, film, fashion and drugs all became a part.

The history lesson will resume in a moment, but it's important to note that consumerism's integral role in the forming and perpetuation of youth culture is on a steady increase. We've reached the stage today where the pressure that consumerism puts on young people has given rise to two types of individuals. We'll turn our attention to the idea of a 'global young person' in due course, but for now it's time to reveal its forebear, one of the greatest proponents of consumerism today, the notion of the 'perpetual adolescent'. It's the 'Peter Pan' conspiracy, if you will, and like most good fairy tales this one spins a good yarn. Whether that will include a 'happily ever after' or not remains to be seen.

In the beginning

Well, not quite the beginning. As we've seen, the 1950s and 60s didn't mark the start of the youth culture story, but it was here that consumerism was neatly tied in with the search for identity most commonly associated with adolescence.

Teenagers began to reject the bland conformity of domestic suburban life in the post-war economic boom. The generations who had lived through the ravages of war and the frugal living that went with it were only too happy to embrace the quiet life and luxuries made available by the ever-growing manufacturing industries. Their children, however, were not. Troubled teens found various outlets for their frustrations, cultural and technological revolutions that provided them with a whole new language with which to vent spleen against their elders and effectively distance themselves from their passé ideals.

James Dean spoke for a new generation in *Rebel without a Cause*. Bill Haley provided the soundtrack for a film and teen riots when *The Blackboard Jungle* made use of the seminal rock classic 'Rock Around The Clock' (on seeing the film, many teenagers began ripping up cinema seats). Psychedelic drugs in the 1960s provided a whole new way of 'seeing' life – a 'neo-spiritual' rebellion – and the Pill paved the way for the sexual revolution.

One perfect illustration of the way in which new technologies acted as a catalyst for youth culture is the impact that the Memphis monarch Elvis Presley had on teenagers worldwide. Elvis's domination of America would not have been complete had it not been for the helping hand of television.

Cultural critics make much of how media not only reflects social behaviour but informs it as well. How the camera treated Elvis is a case in point.[4] On TV shows of that era there would be medium close-ups of Elvis shaking his pelvis. Immediately the camera would cut to extreme close-ups of young girls screaming their consent, rather than showing middle-aged members of the audience in mild apoplexy.

From then on, every teenage girl in America knew exactly how you should react to Elvis and to similar global superstars – the fan reaction to The Beatles when they hit America was far more manic than even the British response. The creation of global TV networks played a huge part in cementing peer affiliations – the first steps in providing behavioural 'norms' for teenagers worldwide. It's no coincidence that the first decade to see television established as a truly global phenomenon, the 1960s, is also seen as the decade when youth rebellion raged most strongly.

The 1950s and 60s have often been dubbed the decades most responsible for driving a wedge between young and old. But however revolutionary they appeared to be on the surface, they were in fact responsible for advancing the cause of consumerism: young people didn't give up their parents' love of shopping, they simply swapped spending habits. They bought out of conformity (same houses, same hoovers, same cars – effectively keeping up with the Joneses) and bought into individualism. The new fashions, the new music, the new drugs all offered them icons of independence with which they could set themselves apart from the drab 'norm'.

The supposed revolution of the 1960s set a pattern that was to be adopted by all the modes of youth culture that inhabited the subsequent decades. What seemed radical at first soon ended up travelling full circle: the language and motifs of rebellion became brands and logos which in turn invited the same staid conformity that youth culture sought to expose in the first place.

So in the 1970s, punk's vivacious cry of individualism and rebellion became barely a whisper when The Sex Pistols' 'God Save the Queen' became number one (even if it was an unofficial number one, due to the song being banned from the airwaves). The sound of the underground had become mainstream and as such could be packaged for other culture-hungry teens to consume.

What was born in the 1950s and 60s was in fact the youth brand: uniform adherence to a badge that suggests revolution, but in fact inevitably inspires apathy. As journalist Gavin MacDonald comments,

> The cult of youth is unassailable. The brightest icon of the church of consumerism. When the angry children of the sixties and seventies railed against an 'establishment' they were trying to shuck off the grey world of their fathers and mothers, a society that expected its dues in the form of work and obeisance. Now that establishment has become the ape of youth. The politics of revolution have been subsumed and co-opted for advertising slogans.[5]

However fresh each new youth culture may appear, all are neatly segregated one from the other by the distinct ways in which they adhere to two arch-deities of contemporary consumerism – music and fashion. And in an age where, paradoxically, individualism and conformity go hand in hand (the clothes and the music we listen to have to be distinct yet similar enough to the choices of our peers in order for us to be accepted), 'youth culture' has become the perfect advocate for both ideals.

As Pountain and Robins explain, today being cool is all about balancing those two extremes.

> In any epoch, although cool will have a particularly powerful meaning for teenagers, as an antidote to their ever present fear of being embarrassed, being cool forms part of a risky series of negotiations about becoming an individual while still being accepted into a group – it's about both individuality and belonging, and the tension between the two.[6]

And so we return to the notion of the 'perpetual adolescent'. As well as being the product of an ageist society that associates old age with imperfection, ill health, death and (in an increasingly single society) loneliness, the 'perpetual adolescent' was also born out of two streams of consumer pressure.

The first is that youth culture epitomizes individualism and freedom of expression – the rebellious spirit – and this can sell anything from soft tops to soft drinks. The second is that as long as people are on that adolescent search for identity, then they're still consuming, buying into those icons of independence – hence the 'perpetual adolescent'. Here's David Lyon from his book *Jesus in Disneyland*:

> The most anxious identity crises tend to occur in adolescence, but it is easy to see how this stage can be exploited by marketers. Artificially delaying the arrival of adulthood, and thus extending the period of identity exploration, is an obvious ploy, seen archetypally in Disneyland but in many other contexts as well.[7]

Sociologist Zygmunt Bauman echoes this idea that one of the drives of consumerism is to keep us on the everlasting search for satisfaction:

> Ideally nothing should be embraced by a consumer firmly, nothing should command a commitment until death us do part, no needs should be seen as fully satisfied, no desires considered ultimate.[8]

Elms was right: we're all teenagers in the sense that consumerism keeps us on a perpetual search for identity.

The global young person

The continuing effect that consumerism is having on today's young can also be seen in the attempts of multinational industry to stamp its permanent mark on the face of youth culture. Enter the idea of the 'global young person': soon indigenous youth cultures everywhere will fall prey to the hegemonic designs of big business the world over. Young people from Bombay to Birmingham will drink one drink, eat one burger, watch one music channel. And in whose image will the GYP be remade? That of the white male European or American, no doubt, as the West tells the rest what's cool and what's not.

It all makes good business sense. It costs money to provide products that will appeal to every niche that exists. Why create a broad range of music styles, for example, when one or two will do? Influence the market so that one type of music is popular, and hey presto! Instant big bucks. That's why the charts are swamped with clone after clone of bands whose music is currently 'in'.[9]

So will our rebellious youth rise up in their millions to throw off the shackles that consumer industry has foisted upon them? Perhaps. That is, if they can find enough time to put down the game pad first.

Apathy thrives as an overwhelming wealth of entertainment choices leave us overstimulated and blissfully ignorant. As youth culture bible *The Face* (now extinct) summed up in an article aptly titled 'Zombie Nation', it's impossible to be bored any more because there's so much on offer.

> If you've always got something great to entertain you, you get lazy and passive – you lose the habit of searching for anything genuinely new or important. When you lose your curiosity about how the world really works you become a mindless zombie consumer.

Consumer pressure today

The church needs to take note of the role that commerce increasingly plays in shaping contemporary youth culture. As the recent Church House report *Mission-Shaped Children* points out, whether poor or rich, young people's ambitions are frequently formed by material aspirations.

> Unlike previous generations, there is no way of shielding children from the physical affects of affluence. Television, advertisements, the Internet and media coverage of the lives of celebrities have thrust a glamorous picture of material comfort into every child's home.[10]

Graham Cray commented in the LICC's *Imagine* DVD on whole-life discipleship that the church has yet to realize fully just how much it has been impacted by materialism.

One way we can begin to assess this impact is by detecting where and how consumerism impacts our young people: how business aims to sustain and develop the concepts of the 'global young person' and the 'perpetual adolescent'. Corporations have more than a few tricks up their sleeves when it comes to keeping the young enthralled, and below are just a few of the commercial pressures designed to keep teens buying today.

Promoting brand youth

First there's viral advertising – finding the coolest kid in school and handing them your product in order to kick off a craze. Then there's peer-to-peer influence – in the 1930s record companies paid young girls to scream at Frank Sinatra;[11] today many bands have 'street teams' of young people who hand out flyers and put up posters.

Many schools in Britain and America have also succumbed to the obvious appeal of having big business fund school activities. In Britain, Microsoft have announced that they're going to sponsor eleven academies in Merseyside. Businesses are intent on playing a greater part in the shaping of British education.

Then there's trendspotting. Research agencies specifically recruit 'trendspotters' within cool urban cliques who inform them which trends are taking off. The following is a business statement from one such company. It acknowledges the shift from an understanding that youth culture describes a particular age group to the idea that youth culture is now about a 'lifestyle choice' that anyone can buy into.

> We acknowledge that youth culture is no longer just a demographic but a lifestyle choice. Understanding youth culture and its progress is critical to business success. Therefore [company name] is based on a business-to-business operational model. In addition, current youth market research is ineffective and inadequate in describing and capturing youth trends. Rather than observing youth trends and behaviour patterns in hindsight, [company name] will

> allow businesses to observe, understand and predict change before it becomes mainstream.[12]

Corporate tie-ins and merchandizing for movies, TV programmes and video games is also on the up and up. On its release in 2003, the movie adaptation of the beloved children's book *The Cat in the Hat* by Dr Seuss, starring Mike Myers of *Austin Powers* fame, was toted as the most corporate-backed children's film in history. There were all the usual tie-ins – T-shirts, soft toys and fast-food specials – but cereal manufacturer Kellogg's went one step further by creating a red-and-white striped cereal in honour of the hat in the title. The corporation feeding frenzy around *The Cat in the Hat* prompted one Californian psychologist to demand that parents boycott the film to show that 'they are tired of kids being sold as audience share to corporate sponsors'.[13]

There's also a focused effort to create consumer awareness as early as possible. This isn't simply to do with the fact that we're more affluent as a society. It's also to do with the fact that today's generation are the first to have grown up within a brand culture. Promoting brands isn't a new idea, but the heavy emphasis on selling the *image* of a company, as opposed to promoting the quality of the goods they sell, is new. It wasn't really until the 1980s that branding took off. Companies realized that they could create a cheap product but sell it at a high price if the image of the company was right.

Increasingly, companies seek to secure brand loyalty at earlier and earlier ages. So, for example, The Spice Girls, five girls with distinctly different characters – 'Sporty', 'Posh', etc. – were marketed much like Barbie dolls, albeit Barbie dolls dressed up for a 1990s market. Such an emphasis targeted them not only at a teen market, but also at a pre-teen market, and soon pre-pubescent girls all over the country wanted to dress like Sporty, Scary or Posh. The knock-on effect can still be seen today with millions of pounds being fed into the promotion of teen pop idols.

So as many of these stars are used to push brands, we enter firmly into the era of 'pester power'. Companies all over the world are acknowledging that the quickest way to a parent's pocket is through whining offspring voicing their demands for Nike over Hi-tec, Playstation 3 over X-box 360, or Postman Pat yoghurts over Bob the Builder ones.

With such an emphasis on brands, it's no surprise that school truancy rates are highest on non-uniform days: some children don't attend for fear that they'll be mocked for not donning the latest brand. And, as many teachers can testify, on non-uniform days children are more subdued within the classrooms simply because they don't want to draw attention to themselves and what they're wearing.

Wrapping up

In his book *Brandchild*, Martin Lindstrom underscores the extent to which businesses today aim to cash in on generations who are becoming more materially affluent:

> No other generation has ever had so much disposable income as this one. So it is no coincidence that this emerging generation has become powerful enough to have a specific allotment in every marketing director's budget.[14]

With so many market strategies aimed at encouraging consumerism amongst the young, it seems that the odds are stacked against parents who wish to discourage the spending habits of their offspring. Finding a balance is extremely difficult, particularly when there are so many positive associations tied in to consumerism. For instance, the personalized gadgets such as iPods, mobile phones and PCs that young people collect give them a sense of being more in control of their own environment, as these are communication connections over which adults have no say. We may not understand why young people get drawn into chatrooms on the net, but the real appeal is that young people control that world – even if it's only virtual – and in some ways they're allowed to mirror the independence they associate with achieving adulthood.

The next section will look more deeply at the issue of peers, but we need to realize that consumerism has become an important part of young people's everyday experience. The most positive aspect of consumerism for young people is that it forms part of a communal story for them. The easiest way into any conversation or peer group is to discuss or own the latest desirable designer item, be it a mobile phone, video game or pair of trainers. In this sense, for young people consumerism is both an empowering force and an emotional crutch.

Challenging consumerism, then, is a difficult task – particularly as our economies increasingly depend on our service trades. But we do have to acknowledge that in turning to consumerism children are simply adopting the mores of adult society. After all, as one recent survey concluded, it's adults who provide 50% of teenagers' income. Is this because parents equate a contented child with one who has had all his or her material 'needs' met? As Alissa Quart in her book *Branded* concludes, 'want' in today's world is all too readily interchangeable with 'need':

> The parents of the middle class millenials have surrounded themselves with brand names and creature comforts and they

> tend to fill their work driven absence in their children's lives with DVD players, Tivo and magazine subscriptions. They have taught their children, now teenagers, to 'need' luxury products rather than simply want them.[15]

If we as the church are to act as positive mentors for young people, we not only have to understand how much consumerism has affected youth culture, we have to recognize how much it has shaped our world as well.

We also have to acknowledge its impact on how we do church. Pete Ward, in his book *Selling Worship*, notes that when it comes to church growth models and packaging and selling Christian resources, the church has not been shy about borrowing ideas from the business world.[16] This entrepreneurial spirit isn't just about how we create and sustain markets for Christian resources – it's also about churches being canny when it comes to service provision. Increasingly, churches are recognizing that if certain aspects of their work, be it provision of youth activities or English lessons for immigrants, are meeting certain local authority targets, then why not seek government funding?

That the church mirrors consumer society in this respect is not necessarily problematic. As the church takes on roles traditionally offered by councils, it has to create sustainability for those projects. And producing and selling Christian resources does provide a valuable way of conveying fresh ideas. The problem occurs when churches end up going the same way as town high streets – all looking identical because they're dominated by chains. There's a danger that we'll all buy into the same packaging and our services will end up lacking imagination and diversity, a point well made by John Drane in *The McDonaldization of the Church*.

We do have to be wary of the pitfalls of living in a consumer society whilst also creatively engaging with it and searching for fresh opportunities for mission. In his book *Spiritual Fitness: Christian Character in a Consumer Culture*, Graham Tomlin argues that the church has a vital role to play in a society dominated by choice and materialism. In an age when we 'construct new images and identities all the time by what we buy',[17] the church can appeal to people's desire for self-improvement – a drive embodied by the growing gym culture – by focusing on its core mission and offering people fulfilment that can be found nowhere else.

> If churches became known as places where you could learn how to love, to trust, to hope, to forgive, to gain wisdom for life, then they might begin to be attractive, perhaps even necessary places to belong to. Paradoxically, it is not making Christianity easier to follow that will help it thrive again, but making it harder. Only a distinct form of discipleship that offers real transformation will seem worth it.[18]

We have to have our end goal in sight: our goal is not simply to attract young people in their droves to our churches, but to make young people into disciples. American youth worker Mark Oestricher comments that our response to consumerism should not be to build bigger, flashier churches stacked with the latest in multimedia in order to act as a magnet to young people. That won't help them challenge societal norms: 'It's rather useless to challenge teenagers on their materialism if our entire ministries are built on treating them as consumers.'[19] The discipleship programmes we employ need to help young people engage critically with a deeply materialistic culture.

So we need to address our addiction to consumerism in order to compete with it. The shallow ideals of consumerism hold little value when it comes to offering lasting satisfaction, but has its impact on church left us with a hollowed-out experience of Christianity?

Consumerism isn't the only competition the church faces, though. The most powerful draw for young people today isn't simply the allure of 'cool rules', but also 'cool cliques'. Can we challenge the impact of peer pressure?

Notes

1. *The Times*, October 2006.
2. D. Pountain and D. Robins, *Cool Rules*, p. 26.
3. P. Flynn, in *I.D. Magazine*, May 2005.
4. A. Bennett, *Cultures of Popular Music*, pp. 13–15.
5. G. MacDonald, *Flux* magazine, April/May 2002.
6. Pountain and Robins, *Cool Rules*, p. 22.
7. D. Lyon, *Jesus in Disneyland*, p. 12.
8. G. Tomlin, *Spiritual Fitness*, p. 9.
9. T. Udo, Brave Nu World, *The American Rock Counter Revolution*.
10. M. Withers, *Mission-Shaped Children*, p. 7.
11. A. Quart, *Branded*, p. 49.
12. Taken from the now defunct webzine, www.Mutationspotting.com.
13. *Washington Post*, November 2003.
14. T. Sudworth, *Mission-Shaped Youth*, p. 22.
15. Quart, *Branded*, p. 46.
16. P. Ward, *Selling Worship*, p. 4
17. Tomlin, *Spiritual Fitness*, p. 12.
18. Ibid.
19. M. Oestricher, 'Material World', *Youthwork*, 2006.

3. SWAPPING LOYALTIES: THE RISE OF PEER INFLUENCE AND YOUTH MANAGEMENT

> You have to try and kill your elders . . . we had to develop a whole new vocabulary, as indeed is done generation after generation. To take the recent past and restructure it in a way that we felt we had authorship of . . . that was our world, not the hippie thing. It all made sense to me. It was a uniform for an army that didn't exist.
>
> (David Bowie on the Ziggy era)[1]

As David Bowie's comment illustrates, the voice of the young rebels not simply against adults and elders, but also against youth movements deemed past their sell-by date. For David Bowie in 1971, the 'hippie thing' had already become redundant and passé.

It makes perfect sense that such 'civil wars' between subcultures exist. The youth cultures of the 1950s and 60s had originally come into being through the creation of a strong sense of identity via a language and social experience that stood apart from all others. In order to perpetuate itself, youth culture needed to keep re-emphasizing that sense of dissonance with the world at large. In the late 1970s, therefore, the punks decried not only hippie culture ('Never trust a hippie,' said Johnny Rotten), but also the glam 'sham' rock of the early 70s and the pop dinosaur prog rock bands of the early to late 70s. Pink Floyd was out, and punk was in.

Subcultures of youth

Not all youth 'fads' burn out and fade fast. Some, with a little makeover work, survive the satirical attacks of their peers.

Heavy metal as a youth movement has been around for three and a half decades and is more popular than ever. The world of Ozzy Osbourne and Iron Maiden is just one example of a successful youth subculture – the divergent trends that split young people into groupings of their peers according to differing tastes in fashion and music. Heavy metal's success lies in its ability to create for its followers a language and look that are truly unique. Creating such a dialect and style is essential to the survival of any subculture.

It has often been commented that these variant groups of youth cultures constitute a new form of tribalism: so today we have the 'tribes' of chavs, street rats, grungers, emo kids, trackies and skaters, to name but a few.

Why are subcultures still popular? When asked, 'Why do young people commit crime?' one teenager responded, 'Kids commit crime because there's no sense of community any more.'[2] Just as gang culture can give a minority of young people a place to belong, so youth subcultures also lend to young people a sense of community that society as a whole can no longer offer.

Youth culture commentator Darren Garratt notes that most youth subcultures are formed in order to give some unifying sense of identity within a society where young people essentially feel alien:

> For most young people, sub-cultures are probably, at best, nothing more than a means to create and establish an identity in a society where they can find it difficult to locate a sense of self . . . 'youth' goes someway towards bridging the gap between the dependency of childhood and the independent 'freedom' of adulthood, and in order to combat the marginal social status and sense of powerlessness attributed to 'youth', it becomes its own social institution with its own codes and

> cultural claims. As a result, it poses a threat to the accepted norms of adult society. 'Youth' is therefore the point where the dominant culture loosens the control of the young and 'youth culture' is the result.[3]

Here Garratt hits upon a major point in understanding and re-evaluating relationships between young and old: namely that the distinctions between children and parents are marked by a contrast between dependence and independence. The journey from childhood to adulthood has often been observed as one long journey from dependence to independence. The perceived rebellion that occurs within youth culture is when 'children' express independence prior to being accepted by society at large as 'independent adults'.

From child to adult?

The problem is, when do children become adults exactly? When do they become independent? A consumer society empowers young people to express independence, through choices in fashion, mobile phones, etc., from earlier and earlier ages. However, the boundaries become blurred because, while they're making many 'independent' choices, they're still dependent on their parents.

We'll deal with the blurring of boundaries between childhood and adulthood in more detail in chapter 5, but it's worth noting here its impact on peer 'bonding'. One distinct way in which the lines have been merged is the way society nurtures independent decision-making for children from an ever earlier age. For example, as I mentioned in the last chapter, toddlers can now make consumer choices about what type of yoghurt they want.

If this is the case, is it any wonder that when the outcome of consumer decisions has a greater consequence – 'Will buying these trainers lead to rejection or acceptance by my peers?' – there is increased conflict between parent and child? The conflict occurs not just because children feel that the parents are out of touch, but also because their independence, once encouraged, is now seen as being restricted. The tension arises from children seeing themselves as independent while parents see them as dependent.

Within a consumer culture there's increasing pressure on parents to encourage children's individuality and independence: a pressure that allows children to make more decisions for themselves and provides them with the means to create and influence their own environment.

Connected cocooning

Any teenager's bedroom becomes a prime example of this. One survey concluded that 80% of 5- to 16-year-olds in the UK have a TV in their bedroom.[4] Many also have their own computers with connections via the internet to virtual worlds that they can control (three out of four children have access to the internet at home; one in three children who use the internet make friends online[5]). They also have mobile phones that connect them to peers rather than parents. It's no wonder that when parents seek to impose their own ideas on these environments, their suggestions are often scorned. Music channel MTV has even coined a phrase to describe the way in which young people today can create and experience virtual communities through the technology available in the bedroom: 'connected cocooning'.

As we saw in the last chapter, brands may provide identity, but technology helps create independence. Again it's a balance between the two, but just as it's vital for teens to align themselves with the best brands, it's also vital that they remain hooked up to the latest technology. A recent piece of MTV-funded research on the 'MTV generation' confirms this:

> [The] young have become used to instant gratification . . . Globalisation and consumerism do not deter. Instead Brands define and give a sense of belonging. Devices and their uses displace the real and the virtual, creating a world where you can be who you want to be. And joining the digital march isn't just a personal choice; to play a part in the youth society, it is imperative to be switched on, charged up and always connected.[6]

Adults can't offer young people the independence that new technologies afford them. Children are becoming more autonomous from the adult world and, in direct correlation, are becoming more dependent on peer acceptance.

In a sense children are often treated as adults and children simultaneously: control is given to them, but then demanded back. One reason why peer relationships are strengthening is that friendship groups often tend only to confirm the validity of the independent decisions that friends make rather than to challenge them.

Empowering peers

The peer group therefore becomes a place of empowerment for many young people. It provides a space where personal decisions are affirmed rather than questioned. This, after all, is the 'friends' society, where the traditional notion of wisdom passed down from elders has been supplanted by peer-generated knowledge.

As the following quote from a teenage girl illustrates, parents have little to offer today's generation in terms of advice:

> 'I don't talk to my parents about anything!' Becky exclaims shocked at the suggestion. 'Not about sex or anything like that. I mean I tell my mum quite a lot because then she'll trust me. But there are some things – they're so old I don't think they'd understand.' Most of their parents, it turns out, are in their late thirties or early forties.[7]

It seems that the peer group has become as important as family to many young people. There's a whole host of reasons for this, but one of the main causes is rooted in the conflicting social forces that seek to 'manage' and influence young people: family, media, education and industry. Family and education may wish to exert restraint on the young, while the media and industry wish to encourage independence and rebellion – at a price.

Us and them: the management of youth and the selling of teen rebellion

There's a much used quote from teen epic *The Wild One*, delivered by Marlon Brando's character Johnny Strabler. When asked, 'What are you rebelling against?' his simple answer is, 'What have you got?'

A great deal of political and media discourse today obsesses over how we manage youth. If society deems that we're going down the tubes, then the discourse largely revolves around where we've been remiss in how we raise young people. This quote from Christine Griffin, cited in chapter 1, bears repeating:

> Young people are assumed to hold the key to the nation's future, and the treatment and management of youth is expected to provide the solution to a nation's problems from

> drug abuse, hooliganism and teenage pregnancy to inner city riots.[8]

Griffin picks out a common thread within industrialized society's attitude to youth, exemplified by the British Empire's desire to perpetuate itself. She uses the term 'management of youth' to refer to an implicit, if not explicit, approach to the creation of better societies. Certainly, management of youth was used to try to maintain the boundaries of European empires. Now, however, there's only one superpower left, and the empires young people are required to maintain are those of multinational corporations.

At first the advance of industry created a blip that weakened our ability to 'manage' youth. Much economic development within the twentieth century was dominated by Fordist principles.[9] Motor car producer Henry Ford was seen as the godfather of the production line factory. These factories produced goods *en masse*, cheapening production and providing job security for life. However, two effects of Fordism helped relinquish society's 'hold' on youth – namely the erosion of a skilled work force twinned with the need to provide a market for mass-produced goods.

Assembly lines required little skill and so traditional jobs that had provided strong generational links in the form of apprenticeships diminished. Also the monotony of assembly line work and the service sector jobs that accompanied the growth of capitalism and consumerism provided an 'aspiration deficit' for whole generations.

As the blue-collar blues songs of Dylan through to Springsteen attested, no one aspired to be a factory worker or checkout attendant. The generation represented by James Dean was also jealous of the heroic 'careers' that their fathers had found as soldiers during World War II. In this light, becoming bankers and TV salespeople had little appeal. What did appeal, however, were the lifestyles offered by the boom in the mass-media, leisure and entertainment industries.

Through the promotion of global media gods such as Elvis, the mass media encouraged disquiet and provided a voice with which to rebel against older generations. Through the marketing of such rebel icons, the mass media also provided a means by which, eventually, youth markets could be commanded.

When Elvis and Dean came along, industry leaders got hooked on selling rebellion to youth. They're still hooked, but rebellion doesn't appeal unless there's something to rebel against. This is why so much of youth culture is still marketed by driving a wedge between adult and youth worlds, whether that's via the alternative goth rock of Marilyn Manson, or through films whose protagonists are teen malcontents (*Donnie Darko* is the new *Rebel without a Cause*). This is why there's still an 'us and them' mentality between the generations.

Moral panics

It has to be remembered, however, that if film and record companies sell rebellion to teens by promoting controversial icons, then conversely the news media sell 'moral panic' to a middle-aged populace perpetually shocked at the values of new youth. Everybody has something to gain from teen rebellion.

'Moral panic' refers to the stock shock reaction of media to developments in youth culture. From Mick Jagger being caught with cannabis in the 1960s to Leah Betts's death from taking Ecstasy in the 1990s, the exploits of youth have always received media attention that's disproportionate to the nature of the incident. It's not that the death of a young person from drug abuse isn't shocking or tragic – it's rather that thousands of adults die from alcohol and nicotine abuse each year and this is hardly mentioned.

A recent MORI poll concluded that three out of every four stories about young people in the press are negative. So while anyone can receive an ASBO (Anti-Social Behaviour Order), we more readily associate them with unruly young people. The furore in 2005 over hoodies was a case in point. One shopping centre banned young people wearing hoodies from entering the premises. But as one spokesman for the Children's Society pointed out on the BBC news, we do send conflicting messages to our young people: 'Here you have a shopping centre banning people who wear items that they sell at the centre.'

If recent headlines are to be believed, the ASBO has now become a badge of honour for young people – an act of 'rebellion' that becomes a rite of passage and earns you status within your peer group.

TV and stereotyping

Moral panics concerning young people also occur because we still haven't recovered from the culture clash in the 1960s between generations brought up before and after the media boom – generations that had distinctly different sets of values and moral frameworks.

In that period the media found itself having to straddle the generation gap in an attempt to appeal to both new and old Britain. Indirectly or directly, TV created for the public at large a cohesive portrayal of what the differing 'communities' within Britain stood for. But, in effect, the invasiveness of TV took the creation of social stereotypes to an entirely new level.

As cultural commentator Stuart Hall noted about the role of the post-war media, the 'media have progressively colonised the cultural and ideological sphere'. As we're living 'increasingly fragmented and sectionally differentiated lives, the mass media are more and more responsible for providing the basis for which groups and classes construct an image of the lives, meanings, practices and values of other groups and classes'.[10]

So the distinctions between youth cultures and the adult mainstream became marked: the filtering and all-influential gaze of the media presented youth movements as a threat in a way that could never have been accomplished previously. The media also empowered and sustained youth culture by making young people worldwide aware of what their peers were doing, what they were wearing, how they were protesting. And, as is the media's wont, in presenting young in conflict with old in order to make stories appealing, they set in motion a pattern of 'opposition' that still exists today.

At the time of writing, there's a furore over a report by the Institute for Public Policy Research that once again labels British youth as the 'worst' in Europe. They drink more, have sex more and fight more than their European counterparts. TV news has equated today's youths with the children in *Lord of the Flies*. They're completely cut off from any authoritative adult influence, and so what constitutes normative behaviour or a 'rite of passage' is defined by peers.

Are our young people devoid of all influence from adults, or is this just another example of the 'social amplification of risk', where the negative stereotypes that the media present achieve a snowball effect and become self-fulfilling prophecies? Do we all end up crossing the street when we see a couple of 11-year-olds walking towards us? As you can imagine, they've attached a 'phobia' to this phenomenon – 'paedophobia', the fear of children.

Moral vacuum?

Some would hail the 'Lord of the Flies' phenomenon as an accurate description of how youth 'tribes' are formed today. As youth culture researcher Nick Barham puts it:

> In the 1960s, people were rebelling against the standards of their parents' generation . . . But now youngsters don't have anything to rebel against because they didn't grow up knowing any standards.[11]

Young people have bought into the rebellion motif, but on one level they're simply creating their own systems and rules that just happen to conflict with the adult mainstream 'norm'. As long as the group accepts a certain form of behaviour, it becomes legitimate even if (or in some cases precisely because) it's illegal.

Barham refers to two groups, psychedelic clubbers and petrolheads, who, to the outside world, seem little more than 'hedonistic delinquents . . . [and] certainly, both groups get their kicks partly from illegal acts, whether it's popping pills in clubs or racing cars where they shouldn't'. But essential to both is a sense of belonging where 'for a few hours at least, they can determine their own laws, their own parameters of conduct'.[12]

Barham's book is the result of a year spent travelling the British Isles and talking to young people. It's entitled *Disconnected* and it seems to be an accurate summary of how today's youth tribes dissociate themselves from traditional society.

Conclusion

Consumerism is the most subtle and effective form of youth management. Through youth-focused media channels, it convinces young people that they're savvy and switched on to exactly how they're being manipulated by their elders, but it also provides, for a price, an outlet for teen angst through fashion, music and film.

In considering the impact of consumerism and other societal constraints, we're right to think that young people face more pressures than ever before. Think of the conflicting forces that work together to shape young people's worlds alongside consumerism: media, family, peers, school and technology – all vying in some sense to 'manage' youth. There has never been a more confusing time to be a young person. Is it any wonder that their loyalties often lie not with the forces that are perceived to wish to manipulate them, but with their own peer groups?

How, as the church, do we help young people assess and critique the influence that these differing factors have on them? It's no easy task. It's in the interests of big business to maintain youth subcultures – niche markets to which they can pander. Youth culture has become such a dominant brand that it's difficult to see how we can override it as a cultural story. What do we do once Pandora's box has been opened? As Darren Garratt says, 'Once society has created the "problem" of youth sub-cultures, how does it then find a solution?'[13]

Part of that work is in deconstruction: assessing how the 'conflict' between the ages has been constructed so that we know better how to create solutions. This includes debunking negative stereotypes of youth.

As sociologist Sheila Allen commented way back in the

late 1960s, social change has been the defining force in creating differing relationships between the generations:

> Age relations (including youth) are part of the economic relations and political and ideological structure in which they take place. It is not the relations between ages which explain the changes or stability in society, but changes in societies which explain the relations between the ages.[14]

When it comes to the church, the cracks are beginning to show: the impact of society's influence on relationships between generations has led to a decrease in young people in our pews.

Consumerism and media have had an increasingly disruptive effect on those relationships, and the result is the strengthening of peer loyalties. But their influence would be nothing without the technology that serves them. More than any other factor, technological advance has in many respects created distinct divisions between young and old and has disrupted traditional notions of authority, mentoring and the passing down of wisdom.

Notes

1. *Uncut* magazine, March 2003.
2. *Independent on Sunday*, November 2006.
3. D. Garratt, 'Youth Culture and Sub-Cultures', in J. Roche and S. Tucker (eds), *Youth in Society*, p. 143.
4. S. Palmer, *Toxic Childhood*, p. 257.
5. *Guardian*, November 2005.
6. Ibid.
7. *Observer*, March 2001.
8. C. Griffin, 'Representations of the Young', in Roche and Tucker, *Youth in Society*, p. 17.

9. N. Lee, *Childhood and Society*, p. 11.
10. D. Hebdige, *Subculture*, p. 85.
11. *Independent*, November 2005.
12. Ibid.
13. Garratt, 'Youth Culture and Sub-Cultures', p. 148.
14. P. Mizen, *The Changing State of Youth*, p. 12.

PART 2

MIND THE GAP: GENERATIONAL TENSIONS AND THE CHURCH

4. TECHNOLOGY AND THE TRANSFER OF POWER

> I recently learned something quite interesting about video games. Many young people have developed incredible hand, eye, and brain coordination in playing these games. The air force believes these kids will be our outstanding pilots should they fly our jets.
> (Ronald Reagan, from a speech in 1983)

> Video games are a waste of time for men with nothing else to do.
> (Ray Bradbury, sci-fi author)

Previously I've focused on the idea that at one time society had the authority structures in place to be able directly to 'control' and influence the behaviour of young people, whether that was through strict schooling or established institutions such as the Scouts. However, we now live in a world where the 'authority' of adults is often rarely recognized, be they teacher or parent.

This isn't simply an instance of 'moral panic' (although the stereotyping of youth as 'rebellious' played a part in helping moral panic become a self-fulfilling prophecy). Alienation from adult influence is a fact of life for many young people, partly because of negative connotations of life with adults, but also because of the appeal of youth culture and the expansion of peer influence. As a result we have increasing instances of adults not being able to connect with young people.

A recent spate of suicides in Japan has in part been blamed on this growing sense of dissonance between generations.

Young people being bullied at school see suicide as their only way out. As one worker at a suicide prevention centre in Tokyo put it, 'Children think that adults cannot be trusted . . . they think there is no point consulting adults about their troubles.'[1]

In Britain today, parents are increasingly concerned that they don't have what it takes to bring up children in the milieu of twenty-first-century life. Beverley Hughes, at the time of writing the minister for children and families, referred to the reasons for this loss of confidence in an interview in *The Times*:

> Many parents in the past had a lot more support from families. Families were closer. They had their own mothers and fathers, brothers and sisters, around them. And the speed of change, and the pressures – both on today's parents and the children they're trying to bring up – are probably different. So you've got less support for parents from their families and at the same time a rapidly changing world with a lot more challenges in it than there were . . . [2]

As the TV programmes *Supernanny* and *The House of Tiny Tearaways* attest, parents today have real difficulty in setting boundaries for children. The knock-on effect is felt when children show little regard for any adult who attempts to coerce them, be that in school or in a public space. So why does this dissonance exist? It seems that in many respects the adult world has indeed lost any sense of 'power' it had over the young.

Adults as redundant 'filters'

I would suggest that this 'relinquishing of authority' has largely been fostered by technological advance. As I've already indicated, technology has played a huge part in distancing young people from the world of adults. To a certain extent, adults are no longer their children's main connection between domestic life and the outside world. Their role as 'filters' between their children and the wider world is now largely redundant.

Parents, grandparents, teachers, friends and neighbours once played a central role in dispensing wisdom to the young. It's no longer the case. Primarily through TV, but later through the internet and mobile phones, technology has displaced parents as the primary source of information about the world at large. Media and information technology have become surrogate parents, whether we like it or not, and not only do they teach children independence of choice, they also influence their priorities.

Children today are becoming empowered by their own ability to 'explore' or experience the world for themselves. At one time parents could discuss issues such as sex with their children when they felt it was appropriate. Now parents find themselves in the role of 'wisdom' clarifiers – having to refine and define information on such subjects that has been gleaned either directly from TV and other media, or indirectly from someone else in the playground, who in turn has probably seen it on TV or the internet. Parents are no longer the 'medium' through which knowledge of life, the universe and everything is conducted to children.

As professor of education David Buckingham notes, the notion of childhood itself was constructed around the ideas of separation and exclusion. That is, childhood was defined by the idea that there were things which adults knew, of which children had no understanding and to which they had no access.

> The modern 'invention' of childhood depended on the separation between adults and children, and the exclusion of children from domains of life that were deemed to be exclusively 'adult'.[3]

Now, however, thanks to technological advance:

> Children have increasingly gained access to aspects of 'adult' life, and in particular to those which are deemed *morally* inappropriate, or which they are seen as too psychologically immature to handle. One could point . . . to children's knowledge and experience of areas such as sex and drugs; their experience of divorce and family breakdown; their involvement in crime, both as perpetrators and as victims; and their increasing status as a consumer market.[4]

Again the boundaries between childhood and adulthood blur. Adulthood holds few surprises for young people. What can adults tell young people that they don't know already? The adult voice has become lost in the babble of the revelatory communication exchange between peers.

For example, trading information about taboo subjects such as sex has always been a favoured schoolyard pastime, but never before has it been accompanied by such a wealth of available information or stimulation. The lines between illusion and reality become blurred when young people inundated with sexual imagery attempt to turn fantasy into fact. Today there are increasing instances of schools disciplining young people who have made their own pornography using video phones and then have circulated it round their phone network.

Mobile phones also mean that peers can easily replace parents as the first port of call when they have an issue they wish to discuss. (In the UK alone, 91% of 12-year-olds have their own mobile phone.[5]) Young people can 'filter' adults out of the equation so easily in today's world. Teens in the home are far more likely to 'phone a friend' rather than consult their parents on a pressing issue.

Good advice?

Young people's dependence on each other for advice can also mean that 'wisdom' simply becomes the product of peer approval, rather than the product of experience, and as such is fairly arbitrary.

One youth worker, wanting to prove that elders often do have something worthwhile to say, provided an excellent instance of this. He was taking a school class and gave the 14-year-olds a case study: 'A 17-year-old boy or girl asks you out on a date. Who do you ask for advice?' They thought about it for a little while and then one boy tentatively put up his hand. 'My parents?' he suggested. The laughter resounded around the classroom. The youth worker plied them with further questions. 'Who would you ask, then – an older brother or sister?' They still said no. 'How about each other?' The response was immediate: yes, of course they'd ask each other. 'Great,' said the youth worker. 'How many of you have actually been out with a 17-year-old before?' No one put their hand up.

The information age has allowed us to bypass traditional passed-down wisdom – just one aspect of Western life that Eastern cultures find abhorrent, and with good reason.

One Philippine island found that cultural norms became displaced when, after years of resisting the arrival of TV, they finally caved in to 'progress'. Previously on the island it was the case that overweight people were viewed as highly attractive. This all changed for their young people when TV presented them with the idealized figures of Western models. Age-old cultural norms were demolished in the space of a few months.

TV and choice

The advance of media technology doesn't simply present children with information to which they previously had little access. It also presents them with choices. Nick Lee's comprehensive study on the changing nature of childhood within contemporary culture, *Childhood and Society*, provides many instances of how technology has made children more independent. Parents used to make choices for children, from food to clothing to how spare time was spent. Then TV and the advertising culture interrupted this in a number of ways.

The post-war creation of a number of innovative domestic devices – fridges, freezers, etc. – meant that households could keep and maintain more products than ever before. An increase in available products meant that more and more consumer choices had to be made. Televised adverts helped with the decision-making process, as well as validating the desire to have more and more products within the home. It was the 'keeping up with the Joneses' marketing push that advanced the cause of consumerism in the early days of TV.

It wasn't, of course, just the adults who saw these adverts. Traditionally the father went out to work while the mother maintained the home and made all the necessary consumer choices. However, TV opened children's eyes to a world of possibility – the possibility to influence their parents over which products were bought. As Lee states:

> Mass consumption involved greater consumer choice, and, largely through the medium of television, children gained

> access to information that enabled them to make consumer choices. This gave them access to a degree of independent choice making . . . [6]

So TV adverts sowed the seeds of the 'tweenagers'. Today's tweenies have evolved out of a society that actively encouraged children to make independent choices from an increasingly early age. This was the birth of 'pester power', influencing parents' purchasing decisions through their children. As we discovered in chapter 2, it's now an established strategy for advertising campaigns all over the world.

Again the encouraging of independence amongst the young helped to cement peer ties: the TV generations are the first who could claim emotional and psychological leverage over the views of their parents via consumerism.

The generation lap

Another factor that has encouraged children not simply to think and act independently, but also to see older generations as, to some degree, redundant, is the way in which the rapid growth of technological development has distanced the generations from each other. As Douglas Tapscott notes:

> When it comes to understanding and using the new media and technology, many parents are falling woefully behind their children. We've shifted from a generation gap to a generation lap – kids outpacing and overtaking adults on the technology track, lapping them in many areas of daily life . . . [7]

When older generations need to learn about new technologies, it's often the young who teach them. This reverses centuries of tradition in which the old passed down skills to the young and a trade could only be learned by spending years as the apprentice of a master. Today wisdom is passed up, not down, and this means that youth views old age in an entirely different light. What do older people have to offer the young if they can't equip them for the workplace and they prefer the company and presence of their peers?

Also the growth in the use of ICT (Information and Communications Technology) in schools has, again, transformed the relationship between elders and youth. The teacher used to be the bridge between the student and the world – much in the same way that parents used to be the filter between the world and their children. However, with the advent of web and information technology, teachers often become co-learners alongside pupils. And students are encouraged to participate in their own education rather than being simply docile receivers.

As with the example of the teenager's bedroom, young people are increasingly encouraged to shape the world around them and to provide their own 'filters' or interpretive perspectives on what happens within the world at large. As Lee infers, the introduction of ICT means that children are further empowered to develop an increasingly individual outlook on life – an outlook that has less and less to do with the world of adults.

> ICT education is not so much about children internalizing sets of pre-selected facts and figures, deemed important by authoritative adults, but, rather, focuses on developing children's ability to 'wrap' the world of information around themselves, to filter and manage it for their own purposes.[8]

The role of the adult diminishes and technology enforces the view that young people can nearly always provide for themselves answers and solutions to the problems they face. Peer influence becomes stronger, while adult influence fades.

Pop culture

Another area in which technology has directly and indirectly influenced the rise of peer loyalty is through the introduction and growth of pop culture. Although we've reviewed a plethora of changes that have all contributed to the development of youth culture, the growth of pop culture via the media of radio and TV can be identified as having the single biggest influence on peer affiliations.

The main reason is simply that media is a powerful storyteller. And if culture can be defined as the 'sum of the stories we tell one another',[9] then in the contemporary world the media is chief storyteller and pop culture is the story it tells about youth culture. Like most stories (and as we saw in the example of Elvis in chapter 2), pop culture doesn't simply reflect society at large – it informs behaviour as well.

A modern 'equivalent' of the impact of Elvis is the influence that hip hop artists have on young people's lives. One teenager, when asked why young people commit crime, responded, 'Media is [a] factor. Music videos glamorise the gangster lifestyle and promote things like girls, money and drugs. What they don't show is legitimate ways of how to achieve them, so the illegal routes look easier and quicker.'[10]

Of course, back in the 1950s, it wasn't just young people who were introduced to a montage of domestic news, global events and soap operas, but an important distinction can be made between the generations who belonged to black-and-white TV and those who belonged to colour TV.

For the former, TV was created for and experienced by several generational strands gathered in the family home watching TV together. For subsequent generations, TV would increasingly be consumed alone, a factor that instigated its importance as a 'nanny' or 'surrogate parent'. Tom Beaudoin, in his book *Virtual Faith*, points out that one of the main reasons why young people viewed TV alone was the birth of the 'latchkey' generation. As the desire for material goods grew, the days of men as sole breadwinners for the family diminished. With both parents out at work, children often came home (letting themselves in, hence 'latchkey') to the embrace of the cathode ray:

> This entry into the world of pop culture at such a young age is one reason our generation is unique. Whereas baby boomers also had an intimate relationship with popular media and culture, GenXers found it at an earlier, more critical age and without the familial supervision of previous generations.[11]

Also with the unique ability of TV and video to captivate the attention of the young, it became a cheap babysitter for busy parents intent on finishing domestic chores. 'Listen with Mother' became 'Watch without Mother', and the few hours dedicated to children's programming during the nascent years of TV progressed to 24/7 availability via videos, satellite and now digital TV. Dr David Walsh of the National Institute on Media and the Family is right to express his concern that using TV as a babysitter for young people will in effect create a 'screen' dependency: 'If we orient our kids to screens so early in their lives, we risk making media their automatic default activity.'[12] In an essay entitled 'Say No to Teletubbies', two academics from Harvard went so far as to say, 'Television viewing is exactly the opposite of what toddlers need for their development

. . . young children's viewing should be postponed as long as possible.'[13]

One reason for advocating this delay is that TV nurtures passivity. As one TV critic, Marie Winn, says, there's a law akin to Gresham's Law in economics at work here. Gresham's Law states that 'lower value currency will drive out more valuable coin'. In relation to the effects of TV, Winn surmises, 'A sort of Gresham's Law of Child Activity seems to operate here: passive amusements will drive out active ones.'[14]

With so much dependency on the entertainment media, it's no wonder, as Beaudoin muses, that pop culture has become a 'major meaning making system' for young people today. The non-stop barrage of information, entertainment and commercialism means that young people have become well versed in grabbing meaning on the run, creating substance from what many adults perceive to be superficial. As Beaudoin states, 'Pop culture provides the matrix for much of what counts as "meaning" for our generation.'[15] Media commentator Douglas Rushkoff echoes this: today's generations have a unique ability to 'derive meaning from the random juxtaposition of TV commercials, candy wrappers, childhood memories and breakfast treats'.[16]

Pop culture, although largely controlled, sold and produced by adults, is the voice of youth. It's a world aimed at young people and populated by young people, an environment shaped by their whims and fantasies. As such, it's empowering, not only in the sense that it consistently affirms the values of young people, but also in that its pervasive nature again establishes youth culture as a dominant force within society, influencing fashion, music, TV and ultimately value systems.

The children of Nintendo

The notion of empowerment and control is very much a feature of another influential aspect of youth pop culture – the video game. If ICT has to a great extent usurped adults' role as wisdom givers, then TV and, even more powerfully, video games have largely usurped their role as storytellers.

Stories make up a huge part of any child's world. Children's imaginations never tire of delving into the realms of fantasy. As developmental psychologist Bruno Bettelheim said, 'Myths and fairy stories both answer the eternal questions: what is the world really like? How am I to live my life in it? How can I truly be myself?'

For many children today, those questions about life, the universe and everything are no longer framed within the context of traditional childhood stories of right and wrong. A recent survey commented on how children's belief in fairies is desisting at earlier and earlier ages. Today those universally significant questions concerning roles in life are ever more likely to be answered by MTV, through videos by the girl band Pussycat Dolls or rapper Fifty Cent. However, for large numbers of boys and young men those questions are also often answered by video games. The computer game industry now brings in more money than the film industry in both the US and the UK. Video games created an entirely new phenomenon – and new addiction – by placing the child at the centre of the story. They're at the centre of a world that they control and manipulate, a world that may be very different from the circumstances of life outside the video game.

The video game puts any child in a position of influence and power. Although children may have influence in the home, they also understand that there's often a conflict between their desires and those of their parents and that domestic developments such as divorce are outside their control. Childhood can also often be a time of overt egoism, when children either exert their will at the expense of others (it's their toy, their game, their rules) or sulk when their whims are denied.

Taking these factors into account, it's no wonder that the computer can be seen as an ideal companion. Sci-fi writer Isaac Asimov once commented, 'Kids like the computer because it plays back, it's a pal, a friend, but it doesn't get mad, it doesn't say "I won't play". And it doesn't break the rules.'[17] As Steven Poole concludes in his analysis of video game culture, *Trigger Happy*, 'Video games give you their full attention. They don't ignore you or say they're busy, they concentrate with rock solid focus on what you say to them through the mechanical interface.'[18]

Nolan Bushnell, the founder of 1980s video console legend Atari, identifies that it's the control aspect of computer games that gives them real appeal to kids: 'There is a completely controllable and understandable universe that is predictable. Much more controllable than real life.'[19] Bushnell hits on an important idea here, namely that children actually desire stability and boundaries in life, achieved through repetition and discipline. Video games appeal because they offer boundaries and rules, but also an escape from the uncertainty of life with adults and life with peers. Peers and adults may seek to influence your independent choices, whereas video games only offer you control.

Video games, along with the other trappings of pop culture, including TV, fashion and music, succeed in placing young people at the centre of an environment which they influence, they rule.

Conclusion

Thanks to media and information technology, each new generation is able to construct for itself a world that is separate from the lives of adults, while they still live within the same context. It's a world of MTV and Nike, ICT and DJs, and although much of this world is sold to children by adults, the young take the raw material and create their own rules and social mores.

A recent story from an LICC 'Word for the Week' email, about a girl from a middle-class suburban grammar school, adequately highlights the power plays at work within peer groups and the pressure on young people to conform to 'peer rule' – even when it means going against inherited values from parents:

> A thirteen year old girl on a school trip to a seaside town actively helped some of her classmates to hide shoplifted goods from their teachers. When questioned she talked about commitment to friends, about peer group loyalty, about not being a telltale, and about the fear of being a goody-goody and being ostracised.

Through consumerism, technology and pop culture, the authority of adults has been not simply undermined, but substituted by the authority and independence afforded to young people in today's world. Adult influence over the young has waned. Institutions that once sought to manage and shape the opinions of youth now seek to court their co-operation by empowering them with choice.

In this light, the church has to understand that if it's to encourage the young to stay within its boundaries, then it has to reassess the way it deals with young people. Separating young people out into age groups where they feel comfortable amongst their peers only serves to reinforce their independence from adults.

Churches often make the mistake of ploughing resources into creating a vibrant and successful youth work without focusing on how they integrate that youth work with the main church. It's little surprise that many young people either leave the church altogether, or transfer to youth-based congregations when they reach their later teens. They become so used to youth church based around meeting the needs of teenagers that they find it difficult to cope with 'Sunday' church focused on meeting the needs of families, the middle aged, or mature generations.

In short, youth work empowers young people, listens to them, plays to their wants, but adult church is then perceived to rob them of that power. This 'strengthening' of peer affiliations has a direct impact on church growth. The post-war generations are so used to being separated out into age 'niches' that they now feel most comfortable in the presence of their peers. Combined with the hypermobility of today, this means that if your church is lacking numbers in a distinct age group, be it teenagers, twenty-somethings, thirty-somethings or families, then your chances of attracting that age group are increasingly slim.

Like attracts like, so churches today grow by the snowballing effect: if you've got families, you'll attract more families; if you've got teenagers, you'll attract more teenagers. Twenty-somethings, particularly in urban areas, are perfectly happy to commute to a church that has a thriving community of others the same age. It's not unusual today to find a city-centre church full of 'young people' – people in their twenties – but with a low or non-existent teenage population.

One answer to the issue of 'separating' out our ministry according to age ranges is obviously to integrate young people into 'mainstream' church from an early age. This is something we'll turn to in chapter 9. However, before that happens the church also needs to understand the nature of the relationships between old and young – the responsibilities that the old have to the young, and vice versa.

It's the aim of any congregation to produce mature disciples. In today's world, though, establishing what it means to be mature is no easy task. It's becoming increasingly difficult to define what it means to be a child, a teenager or an adult.

As Chuck Klosterman wrote in an *Esquire* essay commenting on the death of the teen, 'It's not that kids are necessarily growing up too fast; it's that kids are growing up too randomly. The teenage experience doesn't exist; everything they do is either wholly adult or wholly childish.'[20] This is an accurate description, not just for those in their teen years, but for older generations as well. The rampant advance of technology and consumerism has broken down previously established conceptions of 'rites' of passage.

David Buckingham suggests that we have to redefine our understanding of childhood and adolescence.[21] As adults no longer act as a filter on 'worldly' experience, the traditional constructs that separated child from adult are no longer there.

So what are we left with? An amorphous mess where we often juxtapose 'traditional' childhood activities with 'adult' responsibilities. We work hard and play even harder and only reluctantly settle down. The boundaries between childhood and adulthood have been not just blurred, but demolished. As we'll see in the next chapter, providing a complete picture of what it means to be 'mature' or 'adult' in the twenty-first century is an unenviable task.

Notes

1. *The Times*, November 2006.
2. Ibid.
3. D. Buckingham, *After the Death of Childhood*, p. 74.
4. Ibid.
5. *Independent*, November 2006.
6. N. Lee, *Childhood and Society*, p. 76.
7. Quote taken from LICC lecture series by Norman Fraser entitled 'The Net Commandments'.
8. Lee, *Childhood and Society*, pp. 83–84.
9. Quote taken from LICC lecture by Mark Greene entitled 'Media and the Modern Mind'.
10. *Independent*, November 2006.
11. T. Beaudoin, *Virtual Faith*, p. 5.
12. S. Palmer, *Toxic Childhood*, p. 256.
13. A. Sigman, *Remotely Controlled*, p. 4.
14. M. Winn, *The Plug-In Drug: Television, Computers and Family Life*, pp. 134–138.
15. Beaudoin, *Virtual Faith*, p. 22.
16. Ibid.
17. S. Poole, *Trigger Happy*, p. 184.
18. Ibid., pp. 183–184.
19. Ibid.
20. *Independent*, November 2006.
21. Buckingham, *After the Death of Childhood*, pp. 73–74.

5. 'MUMMY, WHAT'S AN ADULT?'

> Whether it is short or long, whether it is unnamed, named or understood through a variety of terms in a variety of different situations, nearly all societies have a period of transition when young people continue a process, begun in childhood, of equipping themselves to be full adult members of society.
> (B. Bradford Brown)[1]

> Adolescence is like a tightrope walk from the secure, safe platform of childhood to adulthood. Suddenly the world becomes a difficult and dangerous balancing act – which the whole world seems to be watching.
> (Hazel, aged 16)[2]

Hazel couldn't be more right. When it comes to teenage life, the world is watching. We've had *Teen Big Brother*, three doses of *Brat Camp*, *Lads' Army* – a whole host of TV shows dedicated to observing the triumphs, but mainly the trials, of being teenage in today's world.

These shows seem to perpetuate the media myth that teenagers are 'trouble' (*Brat Camp*) or that, at the very least, they lack the 'moral fibre' and 'strong character' of previous generations (*Lads' Army*). And from *Teen Big Brother* (which aired in 2003) we learned that teenagers can be as abusive to each other as they seemingly are towards adults. It was interesting to see how they take their cue not solely from adults or peers, but also from the media. The teenage *BB* community made instant judgments about fellow contestants, accompanied by much backbiting. They also began to express how the experience was making them two-faced, displaying angst when nominating others for eviction. All this clearly echoed the adult *Big Brother* series.

When a heavy media focus on teen life combines with our adult obsession with either living or looking 'young', it's no wonder that many young people feel confused and pressured over issues of image and identity during adolescence. It's also no surprise that many feel confused over what it means to be an adult. If, for example, there was little difference between the way adult and teenage contestants of *Big Brother* behaved, should we conclude that teenagers have already reached the level of maturity our society expects of them – or, perhaps more importantly, the level of maturity that TV and the media requires of them?

How, exactly, does one 'grow up'? As one teen put it, achieving adulthood is an unappealing proposition:

> 'Growing up – what a tedious task. Caught between wanting more freedom, more trust and responsibility, yet at the same time afraid of that responsibility and all it and growing up entails, although few will admit it,' said Georgina, 16, of Stowmarket.[3]

Very perceptive. Part of the problem, of course, is that 'teenage' has been so idealized that those pre and post the teenage years also want to be adolescents. Nineteen-year-old writer Sophie Hart-Walsh sums it up by quoting the famous US journalist Judith Martin: 'Once you identify a period of time in your life in which people get to stay out late but don't have to pay taxes – naturally, no one wants to live any other way.'[4] Sophie goes on to say:

> The idea of 'teenage years' turned the concept of childhood on its head. What child, regardless of their circumstance,

> doesn't look forward to a decade of rebellion, enthusiasm, passionate liaisons, energy and independence? As my seven year old brother, when asked the question 'what do you want to be when you grow up?' replied, 'I want to be 15, 16, 17 or one of those numbers because I can just hang out.'[5]

In discussion, one church leader said to me that today's rites of passage for young people involve simply 'looking older than you are'. Attempting to look old enough to buy cigarettes is followed by trying to look old enough to get served in a pub, to buy alcohol at an off-licence, or to get into a nightclub. Sophie concurs:

> Most of my adolescence has been spent trying to work out how not to seem like a teenager – how to appear much older and more mature. My friends and I learnt quickly. Wearing too much makeup and a pencil skirt on the bus in the hope that we would be charged full fare . . .

It's also true, though, that we're in an age of youth envy, where adults try to recapture the responsibility-free period of teenage excess. This means that many adults don't model 'adulthood' to young people, but instead model 'extended adolescence'. As another teen writer, Joshua Stamp-Simon, puts it:

> Society allows parents to be impulsive, arbitrary and to do more or less what they like. This is because parents comprise most of society. It's a conspiracy. Parents get divorced, and then date or even marry unsuitable new spouses as they please. But woe betide the teenager who makes unsuitable friends . . . I have known parents who have flown off with little notice to New York or blithely taken a

> round-the-world cruise, leaving their bereft offspring to fend for themselves . . . [6]

Do we act any differently in the church? Do we have a clear notion of what it means to be an adult within our society? What does 'growing up' accomplish? And is the church any better than society at helping people achieve adulthood?

The erosion of adulthood

Teenagers and children do take their cue from 'grown-up' role models – we're the ones who establish what it means to be adult. But if that's the case, in church, for example, why do we often choose to employ young, charismatic individuals as youth workers? They're often not accepted by the church as bona fide members of the adult congregation, so how do we expect them to model adulthood and build bridges between young and old? This is especially true if we continue to carve out those separate spaces for young people in our churches, rather than allowing them to interact with adults.

Ecclesiastical issues aside, there are many reasons why the idea of 'adulthood' has been eroded over the last century. As we noted in chapter 1, the move from childhood to adulthood used to be relatively easily marked. As psychologist Christine Griffin suggests:

> In pre-industrial European societies there was no clear distinction between childhood and other pre-adult phases of life. The main stages of childhood, youth and adulthood were defined primarily in relation to one's degree of dependence or separation from the family of origin.[7]

Adulthood came with economic 'emancipation' – the ability to support yourself (or contribute to the support of the family) through work or by getting married during your early teen years. Effectively, you stopped being a child when you were able to have children of your own.[8]

Then, in the early twentieth century, came the concept of 'adolescence', when a limbo period of identity struggle became the norm for 'teenagers' everywhere. However, as we discovered earlier, this focus on adolescence served to emphasize the need to control the behaviour of young people (an obsession our society has not grown out of) and established the teen years as the difficult period with which we're familiar today – thus helping to blur the boundaries between childhood and adulthood. 'Troubled' adolescence became one of the twentieth century's most enduring self-fulfilling prophecies. Every parent still expects their child to turn into Harry Enfield's Kevin, and every young person understands that angst is the coda of childhood.

Adulthood used to be perceived as a period of relative emotional and financial stability.[9] But 'fixed' measurements of adult independence such as starting work, getting married and getting a mortgage are breaking down too. Many people don't start work until they're 22 or older. A job is no longer 'for life', and consequently we no longer remain in a fixed geographical location for very long. It's also becoming increasingly difficult to get your foot on the first rung of the property ladder. And with so many children witnessing the break-up of their parents' marriages, it's hard for them to believe that adulthood will offer any more emotional stability than adolescence does.

As I've identified, consumerism and media culture also generate instability by perpetuating the period of adolescent 'identity shopping'. If you're still searching for the real 'you', the chances are that you're going to do that through spending money – by changing your taste in music and fashion, and lining the pockets of others along the way.

It doesn't help that we have no defined celebrations of childhood's end, only confusing distances between legal acknowledgments of 'adulthood'. At the age of 10 you can be criminally responsible; at 13 you can own an air rifle; you can get married and have sex at 16; you can join the army at 17; but you have to wait until you're 18 to vote, buy cigarettes, drink and watch what you like at the cinema.[10] With little tradition in our society to celebrate the journey into adulthood, is it any wonder that teens place great significance on creating their own rites of passage with peers? These rites seek to imitate the perceived 'independence' of adulthood – which may revolve around smoking, drinking, sex, drugs and joyriding. In celebrating such rites, aren't teenagers simply emulating the role models presented to them by a consumerist and leisure-obsessed society?

There has also been a shift in the vocational expectations of youth. It seems that many young people no longer aspire to become skilled craftspeople or pioneering artists, but instead choose to emulate 'personalities' such as popular 'page 3' girls Abi Titmuss, Jordan and Keeley. According to a recent survey among 15- to 19-year-old girls by the interactive entertainment website www.thelab.tv, 63% now wish to become glamour models instead of doctors, teachers or nurses.

We may question the validity of a report produced by quizzing the users of an entertainment site, but it can't be denied that in a world saturated with glamorous images of young women, teenagers come to associate success and acceptance with having a figure that has been enhanced by a surgeon or a computer. It's surely also a symptom of our get-rich-and-famous-quick culture – as celebrated by the National Lottery and *Big Brother* – that teenagers believe that baring all is the most painless route to stardom and wealth.

These are 'adults'. These are the role models that society presents to young people. As previous chapters have uncovered, we can't afford to ignore the influence of media on society.

Interestingly, two such role models and two of the biggest female singers of all time, Annie Lennox and Madonna, have both respectively critiqued contemporary icons and, in the latter's case, her own role in influencing today's divas.

When asked by a reporter what she made of today's singers, Lennox responded:

> There are some bright women . . . but the consensus is that you whore it. That's what it looks like to me. You have to become a sex object. I'm all for erotica, I love it, but the values that I see on pop videos are like soft porn.[11]

Madonna has openly admitted to regretting her overtly sexual celebrity persona. She even places restrictions on what her children watch – banning TV – and on what they wear. Of the lure of celebrity life, she says:

> I know it sounds clichéd . . . but I've had 20 years of fame and fortune and I feel that I have the right to an opinion on what it is and isn't. All everyone is obsessed about now is being a celebrity. I'm saying that's bullshit and who knows better than me? Before it happens you have all kinds of notions about how wonderful celebrity is and how much joy it's going to bring you. Then you arrive . . .[12]

Perhaps it's the influence of the Jewish mystic cult Kabbalah speaking, but Madonna also mourns the lack of values in today's world:

> In America more than any other place in the world you have the freedom to be anything you want to be. Which is all well and good but it only works if you have a value system and we seem not to have one anymore. It's whatever it takes to get you to the top, that's what you gotta do.[13]

It's a point that I'm going to repeat *ad infinitum*, but adults are the ones who define what it means to be adult. Adolescent culture, as much as we berate it, is simply a reflection of the values of adults presented to young people in the home, on TV, on the internet and in church.

This is, to a degree, the experience of adolescents in the West – a shift of boundaries, confusing notions of what it means to be 'adult', contradictions over the 'freedoms' afforded to young people. We've created a 'no-man's-land' between childhood and adulthood and its territorial boundaries seem to be expanding. Is adolescence *the* defining cultural story of today?

The experience of adolescence, however, isn't the same the world over. Is there anything to be gleaned from other cultures?

Teenage experience in the East

The idea that adults reflect what it means to be 'adult' is a concept at the heart of rearing children in Japan and China. In these two cultures there hasn't been a focus on the nature of adolescence until recently. As in pre-industrial Europe, there was no 'in-between' period, something Harold Stevenson and Akane Zusho highlight in *The World's Youth*:

'There was childhood and adulthood. But in itself adolescence did not attract much attention; it was not considered to be a defined period of development.'[14]

Japan still has no real equivalent to the word 'adolescence', but one term it does use, *shishunki*, although not strictly associated with adolescence, refers to 'puberty, and as such it implies a period of potentiality, freedom, and reason, with overtones of the anticipation of an interest in sexual experience'.[15]

In terms of defining what it means to be an adult, though, Japanese and Chinese cultures aim to lead by example:

> Parents in China and Japan subscribe to modelling theory of learning whereby they believe that children learn most effectively on the basis of emulating models . . . Chinese and Japanese [families] are confident of the ultimate emergence of appropriate behaviour by children if parents display early tolerance, provide a positive environment and function as desirable models.[16]

This has an interesting impact on how children are 'disciplined':

> Children's disruptive behaviour is tolerated during the early years of childhood, but by the time children enter elementary school, they are expected to be capable of reasoning and of acquiring appropriate social behaviour.[17]

The emphasis on role modelling has a strong knock-on effect. For example, in the creative arts in Western culture, anything that can be labelled unique and distinct is lauded. The converse is often true in the Far East: 'Members of East Asian societies are more likely to favour repetition and rote learning over innovation and elaboration than are members of western societies.' And as a result, 'a painting "in the style of" a famous painter is more likely to be praised than a painting in which new elements have been introduced'.[18]

Although there are indications that a new period of creative expression is expected to coincide with changing social attitudes in the Far East, the above example proves how strong role modelling in the home actively encourages the maintenance of tradition. Children who are encouraged to follow in their parents' footsteps also learn to admire other adult figures, and so 'old masters' are venerated and not dismissed.

Japanese society also emphatically reinforces respect for the elderly. Japanese youths have created their own slang language which they use with their peers, but when addressing elders they will revert to formal Japanese. Interestingly, Japan was the only G8 country not to televise the Live8 concert that was taking place in Tokyo. It was deemed that politics is an issue for adults, not youths, and so involvement would not be encouraged. We may not approve of such censorship, but at the same time it's fascinating to note the clear demarcation between adult and youth activity.

The implications this has for how Western children are reared will be dealt with in the following chapter, but for now it provides an intriguing example of how different cultures experience the journey from childhood to adulthood.

Part of the problem is that adults have also lost confidence when it comes to knowing how to create boundaries for young people without seeming draconian. In Britain, as one report found, the teens least likely to experience problems coping with adolescence are those from strongly religious families of migrant origin whose parents do create strict boundaries:

> Six of the 36 teenagers [surveyed] were Asian and each was remarkably calm – sorted, they would say. Their families are strong and structured, they live in a defined community and their religious faith means that many of the complications teenagers feel they need to address – sex, drinking, drug taking – are not options so they don't have to worry about them – and they don't.[19]

So is it possible to create positive boundaries for young people – ones that have less to do with them celebrating their rights as individuals and more to do with them acknowledging responsibilities? Perhaps we should encourage them to see that the journey from childhood to adulthood doesn't take them from dependence to independence, but towards interdependence. Adulthood involves acknowledging that, although people have responsibilities towards us, we also have responsibilities towards them.

Rite of way

If young people are to acknowledge a shift of roles and expectations on becoming adults, do we need to mark clearly the exit from childhood and the entrance into adulthood?

The Jewish celebrations of Bar Mitzvah and Bat Mitzvah accomplish this by combining a sense of reaching adulthood with a commitment to follow God's commandments. Bar Mitzvah means 'son of the commandment' and Bat Mitzvah means 'daughter of the commandment', and the terms refer to the Sabbath following the child's birthday (age 13 for boys, 12 for girls) when he or she reads the Torah aloud for the first time.

It's a hugely important time in the life of Jewish families that involves celebration on a level akin to Western weddings. At the celebration the son or daughter is required to give a speech. No doubt it's a nerve-racking occasion for the individual involved, but it means that the event doesn't just celebrate coming of age but, by giving young people such a responsibility, encourages maturity as well.

In his book *Boys Becoming Men*, Lowell Sheppard argues that teenage boys in today's culture would benefit from experiencing some similar form of puberty rite of passage or 'prop'. Most societies have celebrated the entry into adulthood through traditional ritual of one sort or another. In Roman times, for example, during a specific ceremony, 14-year-old boys would shed the garments and jewellery of youth and replace them with adult clothing.[20]

The important elements for most 'props' are risk, ritual and recognition – aspects mirrored in the customs of the Amish communities of North America. They have a coming-of-age experience entitled *rumspringa* (a Pennsylvania Dutch word roughly translated as 'running wild'). It's a religious rite of passage during which young Amish men and women are allowed to leave their homes to explore the outside world. It's an exploration that continues until they decide whether they want to join the Amish church and be welcomed back into their families, or to make their home in 'contemporary' society.

Conclusion

This is just the beginning of a conversation. We live at a time when much communal tradition has been eradicated without anything of significance being offered to replace it. The church, perhaps, might begin by exploring its role not as an upholder of the past at all costs, but as a community that can demonstrate the value of meaningful ritual within our culture. Celebrating the amazing journey from childhood to adulthood would be an excellent place to start.

It needs to be noted, though, that such meaningful rituals need to take place within 'meaningful' communities. Where there are deep communal ties and a keen sense of shared journey, a prop will take on strong significance. The alternative is a prop that could simply become a spectator event which carries no real transformative value for the individual concerned. For example, confirmation within the Church of England could be seen as a prop, but it rarely conveys any true sense to the candidates that they've now become adults in the eyes of the church.

Compare that with the experiences of one church community in north-east England, who celebrate the coming of age of boys by a gathering of family, friends and other significant adult males from the church for an evening of takeaway curry and prayer. A simple ceremony, perhaps, but the gravitas granted it arises from the depth of relationships experienced within that particular church family. If we're to create strong ties between young and old within Christian communities, superficial ceremony isn't the answer: we need adults from the wider church family to take active roles in helping to 'rear' children in a communal setting.

Again this harks back to ideals that were taken for granted when the limits of community life were fixed by the boundary lines of a village. In today's global village, the church could play a vital role in providing a focus for recovering tradition and imbuing it with a fresh sense of celebration.

More of that later. The final point to make here is that our exploration of the blurred lines between adulthood and adolescence in this chapter has served to highlight the sense of confusion felt by a society driven by freedom from convention, but at the same time recognizing the validity of maintaining established boundaries. It's a conflict often illustrated by the turbulent nature of twenty-first-century family life. Does the nature of family life in today's world help or hinder children on their journey towards becoming disciples? Can the Bible shed any light on the contemporary crisis in relations between young and old, parent and child?

Notes

1. B. Bradford Brown and R. W. Larson, 'The Kaleidoscope of Adolescence', in B. Bradford Brown *et al.* (eds), *The World's Youth*, p. 6.
2. *The Times*, November 2006.
3. Ibid.
4. *Independent*, November 2006.
5. Ibid.
6. Ibid.
7. C. Griffin, 'Representations of the Young', in J. Roche and S. Tucker (eds), *Youth in Society*, p. 18.
8. S. Gerali, *Teenage Guys*, p. 20.
9. N. Lee, *Childhood and Society*, pp. 11–14.
10. P. Mizen, *The Changing State of Youth*, pp. 5–9.
11. *Independent*, June 2005.
12. Interview in *Q* magazine, 2005.
13. Ibid.
14. H. W. Stevenson and A. Zusho, 'Adolescence in China and Japan: Adapting to a Changing Environment', in Bradford Brown *et al.*, *The World's Youth*, p. 142.
15. Ibid., p. 143.
16. Ibid., pp. 144–145.
17. Ibid.
18. Ibid., p. 155.
19. *The Times*, October 2003.
20. L. Sheppard, *Boys Becoming Men*, pp. 13–14.

6. FAMILY LIFE AND DISCIPLING YOUNG PEOPLE

> The family and its maintenance really is the most important thing not only in your personal life but in the life of any community, because this is the unit on which the whole nation is built.
> (Margaret Thatcher)[1]

> Indeed for what purpose do we older folks exist, other than to care for, instruct and bring up the young?
> (Martin Luther)[2]

As a young person, what would Jesus do?

> After three days they found him in the temple courts, sitting among the teachers, listening to them and asking them questions. Everyone who heard him was amazed at his understanding and his answers. When his parents saw him, they were astonished. His mother said to him, 'Son, why have you treated us like this? Your father and I have been anxiously searching for you.'
>
> 'Why were you searching for me?' he asked. 'Didn't you know I had to be in my Father's house?' But they did not understand what he was saying to them.
>
> Then he went down to Nazareth with them and was obedient to them. But his mother treasured all these things in her heart. And Jesus grew in wisdom and stature, and in favour with God and men.
> (Luke 2:46–52)

Luke is the only Gospel writer to relay this incident at the temple, so we have him to thank for pointing us to the only 'youth ministry' Jesus ever received that's actually recorded.[3] The teachers in the temple may not have considered themselves to be youth workers, but they certainly had no qualms in encouraging the faith of their young visitor.

This unique episode in the early life of Christ actually helps us to identify a positive model for discipling young people. It also helps to outline, through comparison with our contemporary context, some of the difficulties involved in bringing young people to maturity in faith.

On a positive note, this is a clear example of wisdom exchange between generations: Jesus finds elders who actively listen to the questions he has to ask. Although stunned by the brilliance of his questioning, the elders in the temple would have had the necessary knowledge and wisdom to address his questions. This is probably why Jesus stayed behind, to make the most of their expertise. In looking for answers he knew his parents couldn't provide, Jesus was able to find a context where other significant adult figures could teach him – indicating a communally felt responsibility to respond to the questions of youth. Finally, respect underpins the wisdom exchange. Christ respects the views of those he questions, and his mentors respect his questions.

As Glenn Miles points out, that one line in Luke 2:52, 'Jesus grew in wisdom and stature, and in favour with God and men', highlights four different areas in which Christ matured. 'Jesus developed mentally (wisdom), physically (stature), in favour with God (spiritually) and in favour with men (socially).'[4] These are four areas that shouldn't be neglected as we seek to encourage the development of our young people.

So in Luke we have a perfect model for discipling young people. It's a method that doesn't employ specialist youth workers to impart knowledge or act as spiritual mentors on behalf of the rest of the religious community. Note also that there's no shirking of the responsibility to answer and encourage a faith that's actively inquisitive, even when difficult questions are raised. Further, the elders in the temple aren't imparting this knowledge to a mere child. Jesus at the age of 12 is only one birthday away from becoming an adult and this changes the dynamic of the relationship between the parties: they give their knowledge freely to assist his growth in spirit and maturity.

Things have changed, you might say, and you'd be right. We've been through a couple of millennia of change. Comparing the task of nurturing faith amongst the young today with the above example from Jesus' time might have us identifying the following problems – problems with which we'll be familiar from previous chapters.

The fact that there's no longer any assumption that adults are authorities when it comes to any subject – be it fashion or faith – makes conveying truth challenging. There are also fewer and fewer contexts in which young people choose to, or actually can, listen to the voice of adults, and vice versa. And society, the church included, is obsessed with addressing niche age groups in order to appeal to the specific needs and wants of the group demographic. This is as true of the church youth group as it is of MTV and media marketing. Is it any wonder that young people who are so used to hearing the voices of their contemporaries prefer to listen to peer-generated 'wisdom' rather than the passed-down wisdom of adults? When it comes to the generation gap, the questions raised by young people today seem so markedly different from the questions asked by older generations in their youth, that adults often feel ill-equipped to communicate to today's generations.

What's our role?

I'll address some of these issues in more depth shortly, but before we progress it's important to draw another conclusion from the incident at the temple. In Jesus' day there was a clear distinction between child and adult. Adolescence hadn't been 'invented' then, so no boundary blurring had occurred. This meant that the elders at the temple knew exactly what their role was in relation to a 12-year-old Jewish male about to become an adult.

We're no longer so sure of our roles. As a result, we no longer know what 'wisdom' to apply when confronted with an 8-year-old girl who dresses like a 16-year-old, or a 7-year-old boy who demands the latest greatest mobile phone for his birthday. And how do we respond to a teenager who gets pregnant? Is she 'getting into trouble', or just doing something perfectly acceptable in most pre- and some post-industrialized cultures? Wasn't Mary most likely pregnant with Jesus at the age of 14? The difference is, of course, that we don't consider 14-year-olds to be 'adults' within our culture. We're not that sure about 16-, 18- or 21-year-olds either. And how about all those early thirty-somethings who haven't settled down yet – who haven't married, had a baby, or even left home? Are they adults?

I make this case because how we view our 'youth', as kids, as adolescents and as young adults, will entirely shape how we disciple young people – how and what we choose to teach them. For example I often use the following quote by David Wilson of Agape, the campus evangelism organization:

> Teenagers are being taught nuclear physics at school and gentle Jesus meek and mild on a Sunday. No wonder so many drift away from Christianity when they get to university.

When do we think young people are capable of dealing with difficult questions of faith? When do we think they're ready for more robust presentations of doctrine?

Confusion over what constitutes adulthood in today's world leaves us with an indistinct target to aim for: at what age does someone become a mature, active member of the church? If we're adults at 20, why do we need to join the twenty-something housegroup and not one frequented by people from a non-specific age range?

Before presenting some solutions to this issue, it's vital that we focus on some of the other root causes of the blurring of boundaries between childhood and adulthood: changing relationships in the family and a subsequent deterioration of communication between adults and children.

'Cradle' period

It may sound pat, but part of providing the solution when it comes to effectively discipling young people does lie in correctly identifying the size and nature of the problem. So the church has to realize that it finds itself at a unique time in history regarding the challenges presented to familial relationships and the subsequent impact on the development of young people. Never before have peer group affiliations so usurped family loyalties and ties. Never before has there been such a communications breach between generations, with young people unwilling to communicate or spend time with elders, and elders, when actually willing to spend time with young people, feeling unable to relate to them.

This is fairly understandable. Communities throughout the ages have thrived due to their ability to participate in and listen to shared stories. Today there's a myriad of shared stories to choose, very few are ubiquitous, and very few bind us together as they did in the past. Young people watch MTV, listen to Radio 1 or surf the internet for their stories. Older generations choose different channels; they can tell stories to which everyone their own age can relate, from significant cultural events, from World War II, or the Queen's Silver Jubilee.

Although young people today can share common 'cultural' stories, whether it's 9/11 or the war in Iraq, their approach is different. There's a shared cynicism towards history-making events and those at the centre of them. We no longer live in a world where men would rush to almost certain death, as they did in World War I, for king and country. Things have changed indeed.

Neil Postman, in his book *The Disappearance of Childhood*, compares this period of recent social upheaval to a previous period in history when the pace of cultural change rapidly accelerated – the Reformation. He notes that the first fifty years of tumultuous change after the invention of the printing press in 1440 came to be referred to as the *incanabula*, which is Latin for 'cradle period'.[5] We too find ourselves within a period of cultural infancy, given birth to by the rise of communication technologies after World War II.

Surrounded by so much cultural chaos and so many shifts in attitudes, it's unsurprising that the church responded to the communication gap between generations by employing specialists who could speak a language incomprehensible to most – the language of 'youth'. It was an answer to one gnawing question about the future of the church: how do we reach and keep young people?

Nonetheless, while youth work does provide a vital link with young people, in many respects it serves to separate children from the adult population. Of course they come into contact with adult leaders within youth groups. But is it those leaders' express purpose to model what it means to be mature disciples, or is their role, as has been suggested before, to be 'moral guardians', simply keeping Christian young people in a safe place away from the 'negative' influences of the world at large? Is our children's ministry little more than a 'holding exercise',[6] a frail attempt to keep our children occupied at church until they (hopefully) join the adult congregation?

Separate worlds

Is the church in fact creating a succession of 'safe places' for young people – safe from the parents' perspective because there's little contact with life outside the church, and safe from the young people's perspective because their needs are catered for and they don't have to have any contact with the mainstream adult church?

Creating separate worlds for children, young people and adults is a trend firmly established in today's industrialized societies. As we've seen, the worlds of the computer game, the mobile phone and the internet all provide distinct spheres for young people that are rarely impinged upon by adult influence.

Often, however, the difference between adult and child worlds today isn't the amount of time adults spend with young people. Rather, what has changed over the course of the nineteenth and twentieth centuries is how that time is regulated and spent. As history professor John Gillis comments, 'Children's spaces are increasingly "islanded", separated from one another and from the adult world. Many childhoods are insulated from the adult world.'[7] In pre-industrial societies children would be in contact with adults in work and in worship – for instance, children would be working alongside adults, or the homestead itself was the place where adults worked.

Today the workplace and home largely remain separate. We're also aware that both parents spend more time away from home due to the pressures of needing to work. Because time at home or time with children is limited, such time is often not adult focused, but child focused. Activities are centred on children's timetables. Saturdays are spent taking children to football practice or dance classes, or simply doing things that kids want to do – going to the cinema, McDonalds, theme parks or playgrounds, etc. Often, therefore, when children spend time with adults, they don't enter the adult world, but a world constructed for their benefit by adults.

The term 'quality time' often means time when parents serve the expectations of children. Such a focus can be a result of the overt awareness generated in our society about the importance of the parents' role in child development, or it can be a result of guilt over reduced time spent with children due to work or family separation.

Obviously this has an impact on how adults model adulthood to children. We're in danger of cocooning our young from certain forms of hardship so that they end up learning plenty about dependence and nothing about interdependence.

Recent studies on child-rearing discuss how many contemporary families have an inability to build up resilience in children. Every need of the child is catered for and children aren't expected to perform tasks around the house, so they don't learn that goals are accomplished through sacrifice or that it's not possible (or desirable) to satisfy their every whim. It has been suggested that such factors could play a significant part in the increasing rates of depression and self-harm amongst teenagers. When teenagers are confronted with an emotional crisis and things don't go their way, they simply don't have the coping mechanisms to deal with it.

The way ahead for discipling young people

So what are the implications for discipling young people? First and foremost, we need to understand that discipling happens best in the context of role modelling. Children learn how to act in the world by seeing how adults act in the world. So in a world where the boundaries between childhood and adulthood are blurred, one solution is that adults need to be adults.

When it comes to understanding what it means to be a mature follower of Christ, children look to adults – all adults within the church congregation, not just the youth worker, not just the minister, not just the parents. We represent journey's end as far as childhood is concerned.

So do we employ a youth worker who's charismatic, energetic and into the latest form of youth culture, be it DJ-ing or skateboarding? Or do we employ someone who isn't exactly like our young people are already – a mature Christian who leads by example, who can build relationships and pass on biblical wisdom to our youth? And can we build churches that celebrate the communal role and responsibility of bringing up children in Christ?

Of course it's true that effective discipling begins at home. And it's no wonder that when they're looking for biblical insight on parenting, people turn to Proverbs. This book exemplifies the role of elders in passing down wisdom to the young.

We may find the attitude of Proverbs to parenting rather extreme. 'Spare the rod and spoil the child' isn't likely to go down well with a contemporary readership. But, as theologian Derek Kidner notes, Proverbs advocates the harsh disciplining of a child for two reasons. The first, as Proverbs 22:15 highlights, is that 'folly is bound up in the heart of a child' and therefore, as Kidner adds, 'it will take more than words to dislodge it'.[8]

The second reason is that 'character (in which wisdom embodies itself) is a plant that grows more sturdily for some cutting back'.[9] As Proverbs 29:15 surmises, a child left to its own devices will only produce shame for the parent. This could be seen to maintain that wisdom is non-negotiable: elders know what's good for the child, and the child does not.

As we've seen, this stance has been undermined in today's world, but only to an extent. Children may think that they or their peers know better when it comes to relationships or fashion, but we do draw the line at allowing children to provide their own syllabus for GCSE exams or to eat fast food all the time.

Perhaps in the church we've negotiated too much with children. We pander to what we believe are the needs of children to the extent that the role of adults as authority figures is diminished. Or perhaps it's the case that adults within the church have been too dependent themselves on biblical teaching being provided for them, and so have little biblical understanding of their own to offer. We have little resilience of our own when it comes to facing the difficult questions that adhering to a faith sometimes asks of us.

The purpose of looking briefly at Proverbs is not to advocate the wholesale reintroduction of harsh discipline, but it does highlight the biblical emphasis on the important role of elders in bringing up children. If the church is haemorrhaging teenagers, we have to ask ourselves if it's because we address the issue of discipleship too late. Is the spiritual education we provide for our young people neither consistent enough nor rigorous enough to provide them with the means to have a strong and stable faith in a time when there are many challenges to the authenticity and relevance of our beliefs?

Inherited faith

Deuteronomy 6 also underlines the emphasis on the communal aspect of introducing faith to the young. The *shema* – the divine imperative central to our faith, 'Love the LORD your God with all your heart and with all your soul and with all your strength' (Deuteronomy 6:5) – is followed by another imperative emphasized by Moses:

> These commandments that I give you today are to be upon your hearts. Impress them on your children. Talk about them when you sit at home and when you walk along the road, when you lie down and when you get up.
> (Deuteronomy 6:6–7)

It's vital that we embrace a vision of discipleship that's holistic, encompassing every area of life. Deuteronomy indicates that celebrating faith in the home is an essential aspect of this, and there's now a wealth of resources aimed at encouraging teaching in the home (see Appendix 2).

Discipling our young people is obviously an essential part of shaping the future of the church. The most important thing in encouraging our young people to develop a well rounded and vital understanding of what it means to follow Christ is to have that passion for following Christ ourselves.

We need a passion that actively seeks to create communities not of convenience, but of sacrifice: giving up time and energy to assist the training of young people in the church, and generating discussion about faith whenever we can at home, at mealtimes, in the car, in the nursery.

Young people and discipleship through the ages

Throughout church history, theologians have emphasized the importance of the family in spiritual formation and also the necessity of providing *catechesis*, religious instruction for the young.

John Chrysostom (*c.* 347–407), early church Father and bishop of Antioch, was concerned that the growing influence of Christianity within the Roman Empire meant that more and more people's faith became 'nominal'. People were becoming Christians in order to secure status and this had a knock-on effect on their attitudes to the young:

> The purity of faith was in jeopardy as Christians increasingly took up responsibilities in the secular world. Belonging to the church was beginning to be seen as routine and advantageous for worldly success. Chrysostom abhorred a cake-frosting variety of Christianity. Constantly he inveighed against the moral laxity of self-professed Christians and their excessive preoccupation with material possessions, entertainment, social status, and political influence. He was especially troubled, even outraged by the eagerness of some Christian parents to propel their children into secular professions while neglecting their spiritual and moral formation.[10]

Chrysostom's critique seems to ring true today as well. Although there's nothing wrong with encouraging young people to take jobs in 'secular' industry (if, indeed, there's such a thing as 'secular' work – see chapter 7), we must admit that a materially driven culture has impacted our ability and drive to oversee our children's spiritual formation.

Chrysostom took the view that the domestic family was a sacred community – it *was* church – and that our attitude to family had deep implications for the wider body of Christ:

> If we regulate our households [properly] . . . we will also be fit to oversee the church, for indeed the household is a little church. Therefore, it is possible for us to surpass all others in virtue by becoming good husbands and wives.[11]

As one of this chapter's opening quotes attests, one of the fathers of the Reformation, Martin Luther (1483–1546), also felt that religious instruction for the young was a central imperative for any church community. He was of the opinion that it was easier to 'form' the beliefs of a child than it was to 'transform' the behavioural patterns and beliefs of an adult.[12] It was a lesson no doubt learned from Proverbs 22:6: 'Train a child in the way he should go, and when he is old he will not turn from it.'

Although 'adolescence' had not yet reared its head, both Luther and his Reformation contemporary Calvin[13] recognized that the awakening of the sex drive had potential to incite rebellion, or at least provide a distraction from spiritual instruction. Luther in particular was convinced that if the family provided proper religious instruction for the child, then the pubescent years, although tumultuous, would not result in the individual turning from faith:

> Luther did agree . . . that discipline and teaching in the receptive years of childhood were crucial if the person was to make the passage through puberty and into adulthood

> successfully . . . catechizing (religious instruction) was important for all ages, but Luther and his followers focused on children as being the most susceptible to formation . . . He saw the family as the natural locus of education: parents catechizing their children and household dependants, joining them in prayers, teaching them their proper duties and administering discipline.[14]

The Reformation sought to re-establish the importance of religious instruction for the laity, both young and old. No longer was biblical or doctrinal knowledge the preserve of those ordained by the church. In order to help laypeople in the religious training of themselves and their families, Luther created the 'small catechism', a basic exposition of the Christian faith. It included explanations of the Apostles' Creed and the Ten Commandments, morning and evening prayers and blessings to say before and after eating.

Certainly it appears that in Jesus' day as well, biblical wisdom was fostered by the whole community. Rob Bell, in his book *Velvet Elvis*, speaks of the serious intentionality of training children in the faith within Jewish life:

> The first five books of the Bible, *Torah* can mean teaching instructions, or simple way . . . Now the question among the rabbis, the teachers of Jesus' day, was, how young do you begin to teach the Bible, the *Torah* to kids? One rabbi said, 'under the age of six we do not receive a child as a pupil; from six upwards accept him and stuff him [with *Torah*] like an ox.'

This was why many people who asked questions of Jesus, and Jesus himself, could quote scriptures off by heart. Bell goes on to quote the first-century Jewish historian Josephus:

'Above all else, we pride ourselves on the education of our children.'[15]

Perhaps it's time for the church to admit that when it comes to instructing our children in the faith, we lack the ambition not just of our Christian forefathers, but also of the exponents of other belief systems today. How much of a Christian worldview do our young people soak up during the week? How much of a secular worldview do they absorb during the same time?

Conclusion

As the incident in the temple illustrated, it's vital that we provide a context in which young people can ask questions about faith and learn not only from the youth worker or pastor, but from the whole congregation. We have to ask whether traditional methods of teaching in the church are adequate. Does the Sunday sermon allow room for questioning and discussion? Is just one voice heard expressing biblical wisdom? Do we address the difficult questions presented to faith in the twenty-first century?

What does church life 'prepare' children for? Are we preparing our children for adulthood or adolescence? Do our teaching styles smack too much of play and not enough of formal religious instruction? And if adulthood in today's world is merely a form of extended adolescence, how do we restore a biblical mandate for what it means to be mature – that is, someone well versed in biblical wisdom and the love of God?

Our young people are growing up in a society where there's a proliferation of worldviews. Questions about the uniqueness of Christ, the authenticity of the Bible, and serious thinking about moral and ethical dilemmas all need to be presented within church. Perhaps when it comes to teaching young people (and adults), we need to take the kid gloves off.

Notes

1. *Daily Mail*, interview 1989.
2. J. E. Strohl, 'The Child in Luther's Theology', in M. J. Bunge (ed.), *The Child in Christian Thought*, p. 134.
3. R. Bell, *Velvet Elvis*, p. 129.
4. G. Miles, 'The Development of Children in their Families and Communities', in G. Miles and J. Wright (eds), *Celebrating Children*, p. 33.
5. N. Postman, *The Disappearance of Childhood*, p. 37.
6. M. Withers, *Mission-Shaped Children*, p. 24.
7. J. R. Gillis, 'Childhood and Family Time: A Changing Historical Relationship', in A. Jensen and L. McKee (eds), *Children and the Changing Family*, p. 153.
8. D. Kidner, *Proverbs*, p. 51.
9. Ibid.
10. V. Guroian, 'The Ecclesial Family', in Bunge (ed.), *The Child in Christian Thought*, p. 64.
11. Ibid.
12. Strohl, 'The Child in Luther's Theology', pp. 144–149.
13. B. Pitkin, 'The Heritage of the Lord', in Bunge (ed.), *The Child in Christian Thought*, p. 165.
14. Strohl, 'The Child in Luther's Theology', p. 145.
15. Bell, *Velvet Elvis*, p. 125.

7. CHURCH AND THE GENERATION GAP: A GROWING CONFLICT AND CHALLENGES TO DISCIPLESHIP

> . . . not only is this new machinery making the young more sophisticated, altering their ideas of what culture and literacy are, it is transforming them, connecting them to one another, providing them with a new sense of political self . . . As digital communications flash through the most heavily fortified borders and ricochet around the world independent of government and censors, children can for the first time reach past the suffocating boundaries of social convention, past their elders' rigid notions of what is good for them.
> (Jon Katz)[1]

> What's done to children, they will do to society.
> (Karl Menninger)

So what have we 'done' to children? Have we placed them within a perpetual playground environment? Have we severed them from any sense of responsibility and nannied them with leisure technology? And if so, is it small wonder that when you reach your twenties and thirties notions of maturity and 'settling down' are often elusive and all that's left is an exaggerated sense of the importance of play? If entertainment has been used as a pacifier and surrogate parent, is it any wonder that 'adulthood' today revolves around the search for new and better forms of entertainment, or else a continued addiction to the comforts with which we've grown up, the familiar glow of a TV or computer screen in the corner of every room?

Part of the drive of this book is to call attention to the fact that we still haven't emerged from the cultural maelstrom that began in the twentieth century after World War II. No one could have predicted the repercussions that the introduction of ICT would have on the world in terms of our notions of geography, space, community and family. Similarly, no one can predict the impact that future developments in technology will have on those same issues.

So this is partly a discussion of how we determine what happened in terms of community and family when the ICT bomb hit. It's about assessing damage: has the baby been thrown out with the bath water when it comes to celebrating young and old living together? If so, what do we need in order to recover?

Holistic worldview

What we need to help our young people develop is a faith that can meet the challenges of a constantly changing world. If we don't encourage our young disciples to create a faith that can stand on its own two feet, then we run the risk that they will distance themselves from the church when faced with intellectual or emotional challenges to a Christian worldview.

In *Velvet Elvis*, Rob Bell suggests that unless we have a more developed understanding of biblical truth, then our young people will inevitably suffer. We've only been taught how biblical truth relates to our spiritual lives, and not how God's truth relates to *everything* that exists in God's wide universe. We've not been taught, in fact, that everything is spiritual. Bell uses the following example to underline this:

> Imagine what happens when a young woman is raised in a Christian setting but hasn't been taught all things are hers and

> then goes to a university where she's exposed to all sorts of new ideas and perspectives. She takes classes in psychology and anthropology and biology and world history, and her professors are people who've devoted themselves to their particular fields of study. Is it possible that in the course of lecturing on their field of interest, her professors will from time to time say things that are true? Of course. Truth is available to everyone. But let's say her professors aren't Christians, it is not a 'Christian' university, and this young woman hasn't been taught that all things are hers. What if she has been taught that Christianity is the only thing that's true? What if she has been taught there's no truth outside the Bible? She's now faced with this dilemma: believe the truth she's learning or the Christian faith she was brought up with . . . [2]

Too much of church today cushions believers from the abrasive critiques of a society frequently at odds with religious conviction. This can be damaging. Sending young people into dominantly 'secular' contexts without preparation is like removing the armbands from a child and throwing her into the deep end. It's sink or swim time.

A recent consultation at the LICC with a leading American youth evangelist, Greg Stier, revealed that many American churches do seem to have failed their young people on this account. Many churches in the US have thriving youth groups, but churches also record huge 'dropout' figures of young people leaving their faith behind when they head off to college.

I asked this question in the last chapter, but I'll ask it again: is discipling in the church rigorous enough? Is it involved enough? Is it engaging enough? Greg Stier cited the discipleship programme of the Mormon Church in America. Young Mormons have to attend discipleship courses often before and after school, and latter teen males have to complete two years of mission work. That's two years of knocking on endless doors, endlessly repeating statements of belief about the Mormon faith, often for 14 hours a day. During those two years the missioners can only go home once, and are even discouraged from attending the funerals of close family members should they occur during that time. They may only convert one person for every thousand doors they knock on, but it's easy to see why this kind of dedication has led to the numbers of Mormons in America increasing by over 100% in the last ten years.

In the UK many children from Muslim families return home from school each evening and straight away start two hours of Koran study. Many Jewish children attend at least one evening a week of Torah instruction.

So how do we ring the changes in the church? How do we encourage young and old to develop a faith that's robust and passionate when faced with the challenges of today's world?

Whole-life discipleship

The answer doesn't lie in simply giving our congregations the right answer to difficult questions: 'If someone asks you where dinosaurs fit into God's plan, then this is what you need to say.' As an LICC colleague said, we're often too interested in providing our young people with 'information' when we should be focusing on 'formation'. It's not about trying to prop up a struggling plant with bamboo canes and added doses of Baby Bio. It's about making sure that the plant grows up strong in the first place, and a plant is only as strong as the soil in which it's planted. Young people may only be as strong in their faith as the community in which they're planted.

It's about helping our communities realize how robust our faith is. It's also about helping them struggle with difficult issues. After Jacob wrestled with God he was given the name Israel, which means 'he struggles'. Our faith only grows stronger through tackling adversity.

The sacred/secular divide

The team at the LICC devote much of their time to helping churches 'wrestle' with some of the issues facing Christians in today's world. The Institute was set up in 1983 by the Anglican theologian John Stott to respond to the criticism that the Christian faith was no longer seen as relevant, and to nurture disciples who applied their deep understanding of the Word to the contemporary world.

Over recent years the Institute has focused its energies on tackling a pertinent and persistent issue facing Christianity in the West – the issue of the sacred/secular divide. This is the view that certain areas of life are more 'sacred' than others, that some vocations are 'full-time Christian work' and others aren't. For instance, we may pray on a Sunday for the work of Sunday school teachers, but we may never pray for the work of high-school teachers from Monday to Friday. As LICC's website puts it:

> The Sacred-Secular Divide describes the pervasive belief that faith is essentially private, church is a leisure time option, and God is primarily interested in some things – such as prayer, social action, Alpha and so on – but other human activities are at best neutral.[3]

This is without doubt due to the dominance of an increasingly secular society. Whereas once the church had a visible impact on everyday life in Europe, now religion has been relegated to the realm of privately held beliefs. And as Tom Sine attests in *Mustard Seed Versus McWorld*, Christianity is marred by a dualism formed through living in a deeply secular consumerist context where worship of God is often supplanted by the drives of materialism. It's an echo of Chrysostom's concerns in the last chapter:

> What we have done, I am convinced, is to succumb inadvertently to a dualistic model of discipleship and stewardship. In spite of all the talk about 'Lordship', everyone knows that the modern culture comes first. Everyone knows getting ahead in the job comes first. Getting ahead in the suburbs comes first. Getting the children off to their activities comes first. And we tend to make decisions in these areas pretty much like everyone else – based on our incomes, our professions and our social status. When we have made these decisions then we sanctify it by looking around for a church where we can feel called to worship.[4]

LICC have produced two journals in partnership with the Evangelical Alliance magazine *Idea* that explore how we can eradicate this kind of dualism – how we can restore a sense of holistic Christian living, or 'whole-life discipleship'. After the latest edition, 'Let My People Grow', was produced, one respondent provided some sage comments on cultural change:

> I find myself reading it in the light of certain other studies from the mid-to-late 20th century, most specifically Francis Schaeffer's 'How should we then live' and Alvin Toffler's 'Future shock'. What is clear from those studies is how comprehensively the shifts in culture and society have undermined the qualities in human relationships needed

> to operate a rabbinical teaching model . . . [so] the transformation from casual Christianity to true discipleship is probably going to be harder for many than their original conversion.

When we invite young people to come to faith, what form of Christianity do we present them with – 'costly' or 'cushioned' faith? The above quote seems to underline that a New Testament view of salvation was one that was inseparable from the individual's growth as a disciple within a community of faith. Jesus didn't simply tell his disciples to believe that he was Lord, believe that he was raised from the dead, and that would be sufficient. He showed how accepting that he truly was Lord impacted every aspect of every relationship.

Inviting people to 'accept' Jesus or 'follow' him?

The view of salvation that we present to people will have a massive formative influence on how they live their Christian lives. So what view of salvation do we pass on to young people today?

Is it the case that largely young people have been presented with 'gateway-style' Christianity: once you're in, you're in, and your place in heaven is secured and safe due to the work of the cross? This can produce young Christians who have a shallow view of the work of the cross and grace, and as a consequence also have little comprehension of what it actually means to live as a disciple of Christ. It's an underdeveloped view of salvation which means that young people may not equate following Christ with a radical lifestyle change.

Laurence Singlehurst, one-time director of YWAM and author of *Sowers, Reapers, Keepers*, has stated that many young Christians in effect become 'enthusiastic dualists': they live two lives, all out for God at the worship service on a Sunday night, and maybe binge drinking and sleeping around mid-week. They adopt different attitudes depending on the peer context, but don't have a concept that their mid-week life is in any way at odds with their Christian walk.

In one way this makes sense to a generation reared on the notion that experience is everything. As Christopher Lasch points out:

> The contemporary climate is therapeutic not religious. People hunger not for personal salvation, let alone for the restoration of an earlier golden age, but for the feeling, the momentary illusion, of personal well being.[5]

Perhaps for many young people faith is only 'tangible' when it provides them with such experiences. Mid-week, removed from the 'heightened' experiences of the worship event, faith doesn't come to bear. The flip side of this is that faith is so closely tied to experience that lack of 'feeling something' is equated to a lapse of faith. So if the worship fails to move you, or you simply 'don't get into it', you perceive that you've become distant from God.

As well as enthusiastic dualists, there are also despondent dualists: those who are all out for God on a Sunday night and make many a trip to the altar for prayer, but feel perfectly guilty about the alternative lifestyle they lead mid-week.

So why do they adopt this attitude? There are, I believe, a number of reasons. One is that worship services often act as a 'confessional'. Many of the songs focus on the work of the cross and repentance, many focus on bringing young people into intimate contact with God. And often these services end with a time of ministry when young people can 'sort themselves out' with God and are reminded of God's character as a loving Father who embraces them no matter what they've done wrong.

There's nothing initially problematic with this, but often young people don't have sustained intimacy with God. There's no personal connection made in their day-to-day lives. They only meet God in a corporate context and so many find themselves in a cycle of 'offending' God midweek and 'sorting it all out' at the big worship event at the weekends.

As a result there's no sustained transformation. You have to wonder if this is down to the model of atonement with which they've been presented. If the cross is simply a neutralizer – Christ's sacrifice cancels out God's wrath – then there's no impulse to progress in Christian faith. The cross has said it all and nothing more needs to be done. There isn't enough emphasis on the cross being twinned with Christ's resurrection – that is, that Christ's life and teaching pointed towards a life that's continually being transformed by a re-engaged relationship with God the Father.

How can we challenge such misconceptions? We obviously need to look for images that restore balance to the full picture of God's work on the cross and the place of the atonement in a wider picture of God's salvation plan.

Similarly, we need to emphasize that the cross is a bridge, not a destination in itself. No one gets their car to the top of the Queen Elizabeth II Bridge at Dartford, stops, gets out and says, 'We've made it, this is journey's end.'

The cross is the beginning of a journey that marks out the rediscovery of what it means to be created in the image of God. It enables us to re-establish the relationship that Adam and Eve had with the Father before the fall. The Christian life is about discovering the abundant blessing God has for those who have a harmonious relationship with him. Abundant blessing. Is that why Jesus chose two symbols of life for us to remember him by – bread and wine, and not a wooden cross? Perhaps there need to be fewer crosses in Christendom and more feasts.

Sin and Superman

So what pictures could we use to describe coming to faith? What 'truth' can we uncover in pop culture that provides a picture of what it means to follow Christ? How do we make the truth accessible to a generation reared on pop culture?

Forgive the upcoming comic book illustration, but it strikes me that superhero stories have replaced traditional myths, legends and folk stories. As such they signify a search for spirituality – or at least a mourning for the loss of connectedness to the 'other', a sense of the transcendent. So when I speak about familiar concepts such as salvation and sin to young people, I often make several comparisons with Superman. After all, Superman's birth name is Kal El. Joe Shuster, Superman's creator, took this from the Hebrew meaning 'Like God'.

In the TV series *Smallville* we see an adolescent Superman slowly uncovering what it means to be a 'son of Krypton' – an alien on planet earth. Only with time does he uncover some of his special abilities. Super strength and speed are noticeable from an early age, but X-ray and heat vision are abilities he discovers only during adolescence. Of course, with great power comes great responsibility and the young Clark Kent, with the help of the loving parents who adopted him, realizes that his powers oblige him to live life in the service of those around him.

I'm sure you can join the dots, but do we encourage young disciples to see that their faith walk is about uncovering what it means to be made in the image of God? What does it mean to be 'as God is' when it comes to living out our faith day to day in service to him and others?

Superman also helps to illustrate the fall. Not many people (apart from comic book geeks) know this, but Superman gets his power from the sun. Cut off from the sun, Superman will not only lose his powers, he'll begin to die. In one story Superman detonates a nuclear warhead in the stratosphere over a remote area. The world is safe, but the ensuing dust cloud cuts Superman off from the sun and he begins to die – not straight away, but gradually he loses his powers and his life. In Eden, cut off from a relationship with God, Adam and Eve lose the 'potency' of life lived in the presence of God and eventually die. As C. S. Lewis once said, 'Once a man is united to God how could he not live forever? Once a man is separated from God, what can he do but wither and die?'[6]

A discourse on the parallels between the Christian walk and the life of Superman may seem like a diversion, but we need to find new ways of establishing what we mean when we invite young people to enter a relationship with God. As I've illustrated, the way we address central themes such as the cross of Christ will influence how our young people experience God.

Evangelism and young people

Deciding what model we use to bring young people to faith highlights yet another generational tension: the role of evangelism. Within the church, the current debate seems to be between (a) proclaimed truth, and (b) provocative praxis. In (a) the gospel is something proclaimed, a message delivered in such a way as to clearly present an opportunity to accept Christ as Saviour. In (b) the gospel is something that's practised, through social action and service, through attitudes at home and work that result in 'provoking' people to want to come to faith. It's the X factor: what has this person/community got that I haven't?

In crude terms, it's like two different styles of fishing. The first is 'fly fishing', where you make the bait so attractive that people can't help getting hooked. The church community becomes such an essential, thriving part of society that people want to experience it for themselves. The second is 'trawling', the door-to-door or street preaching approach where you go out and bring them in. You try to tell as many people as possible about the gospel message and trust that not too many will escape through the holes in the net.

We probably feel that a mix of both approaches is the solution: preach, but make sure you practise. Many Gen Xers, however, have grown up in churches where the former was emphasized at the expense of the latter in terms of social interaction. It was the sacred/secular divide, church good, world bad, and never the twain shall meet except on the church's terms – that is, we only do charity work or 'outreach' in the community if there's some form of gospel pay-off, if it provides some opportunity to deliver a gospel message.

Also everybody but everybody was seen as an evangelist: we all have a responsibility to deliver the message to all and sundry. This raises the stakes so much in terms of developing relationships with non-Christians that it has the negative effect of producing excess guilt and an inability to share the gospel in a way that's relevant and relaxed. It's a form of outreach that seeks to produce scalp-hunters instead of disciple-makers.

In the New Testament there's an emphasis on creating a loving community of believers who live out Christ's rules for kingdom living in a manner that will cause non-Christians to give glory to God. There are relatively few commands for individual members of churches to proclaim the gospel, though it's clear that they're to support the ministry of those who are called to be apostles and evangelists.

So do these contrasting styles of evangelism truly indicate further generational tensions, or is it more accurate to say that the church has seen a shift in emphasis in terms of biblical mandates? Is it the view today that the Word made incarnate was always far more about living out the truth within meaningful communities than about simply proclaiming it?

Ultimately, our doctrinal stance will always end up moulding the shape of the church. But in the years to come, which doctrine will take precedence? Which view of the work of the cross will be at the forefront?

These questions must be answered if we're seriously reconsidering how we disciple young people. In formal terms, we have to establish a curriculum when it comes to teaching youth, and the only way to do that may be through creating new forms of catechesis – a more thorough curriculum of religious instruction.

Does the church understand how much it needs to reassess its teaching of essential doctrine? I'd hazard a guess that, due to increased partnership across denominations and parachurch organizations, and the presence of multi-denominational conferences and festivals such as Spring Harvest, people consider denominational stances on individual doctrines to be less and less important. Are people today more likely to choose churches according to the doctrine they espouse or the 'services' they offer? And how much of 'doctrine' does the average churchgoer understand – or need to understand, for that matter?

An illustration from Alpha will serve here. Recent reports have highlighted that the majority of people attending Alpha courses fall into two groups. The first are those on the margins of the church, or those who attended church in their youth. The other group are Christians who want to recap on the basics. As Sylvie Collins points out in *Ambiguous Evangelism*, if so many Christians need to review essential aspects of their faith, what does that say about the teaching they're receiving in church?[7]

You, me and the kingdom of God

It has become a popular 'equation' in recent years that when it comes to thinking about church strategy, we need to let our 'Christology' drive our 'missiology', and then in turn let our 'missiology' shape our 'ecclesiology'. That is, what we understand about Christ's mission should drive the way we reach out in mission to people, and in turn that will influence what our church looks like – how we live as a community, how we use our buildings. So if we believe that one of Christ's roles was to make people feel they belonged before they came to faith, then we reach out in friendship to our communities without putting any pressure on them to accept our beliefs. Our churches in turn become places that aim to remove barriers: less cold stone and fewer portcullis-like gateways, more light-filled spaces and cafés in foyers.

So what theological framework is emerging to provide a perspective from which we can re-evaluate and reinvigorate the role of church and mission in today's world? For many popular theologians such as Tom Wright, Rob Bell and Graham Tomlin, it's about re-establishing the centrality of the kingdom of God to Jesus' teaching and so to the heart of the church. Essentially, the concept is that Christ's mission on earth can be seen within the context of a returning King laying hold of his rightful claim to be monarch of the cosmos. As one theologian put it, it's a shift from thinking 'Jesus came to preach the good news of salvation' to 'Jesus came to preach the good news about the kingdom of God'.

Indeed, the kingdom of God is so central to Christ's teaching that the disciples spent forty days in 'kingdom of God school' before Christ ascended (see Acts 1:3). The most quoted piece of Old Testament scripture in the New Testament is David's prophecy from Psalm 110 about the establishing of the throne of Christ. For Paul, salvation is a creed that demonstrates fealty to Jesus as sovereign. As he writes in Romans 10:9, 'If you confess with your mouth, "Jesus is Lord," and believe in your heart that God raised him from the dead, you will be saved.'

As Graham Tomlin writes, the church is therefore defined as a community committed to living out the principles of Christ's rule and teaching:

> Jesus probably envisaged small cells of followers meeting in the towns and villages of Israel, living out the way of life he had taught, centred upon loyalty to himself, mutual forgiveness and love foregoing the option of armed resistance to the Romans . . . [8]

So mission is simply seen as an intrinsic part of following Jesus' dictum that the Father's will be done on earth as it is in heaven. As Tom Wright explains, much Jewish observance of the law revolved around the idea of trying to make earth like heaven.[9] For the Jews, the closest representation they had of heaven on earth was the temple, so doing God's will meant emphasizing laws of purity and ritual. For Christ, however, doing God's will on earth – in effect making earth like heaven – meant applying the heart of the law to everyday life. The heart of the law was this: 'Love the Lord your God with all your heart and with all your soul and with all your mind . . . Love your neighbour as yourself' (Matthew 22:37, 39). Evangelism, then, as Tomlin observes, is simply inviting others to live with Christ as Lord.[10]

In a society where Christianity is seen as a worldview that has been tried, tested and found wanting, surely one of the best ways forward for the church is to do a little fly fishing. Presenting a community centred on Christ's selfless ideals will not only attract people to the X factor they've been missing, it will also be one of the only ways to undermine the often misguided but immensely powerful cultural concepts that dominate most people's view of Christians.

A new monasticism?

It seems that the churches that are truly transforming Britain are those whose members are making their private, public and communal lives centre on living with Christ as Lord. This is the simplest answer to every problem facing the church in terms of the challenges presented by the modern world. It's also the most difficult to put into practice.

The future of the church lies in the hands of those who are upping the ante when it comes to being disciples: groups of Christians who focus on the devotional life within a communal setting, living, eating and breathing Christ within a shared geographical locale and committed to serving the people among whom they live.

The Eden Project in Manchester is one such example, as is The Simple Way, a church in Philadelphia. They're part of a movement in the rich West that's being labelled 'the new monasticism'. Shane Claiborne, founder member of The Simple Way and author of the 2006 book *The Irresistible Revolution*, was one of six students from Eastern University who decided to move permanently into an impoverished suburb in Philadelphia.

Are communities like these the way forward for the church? Not only are they grasping hold of the tenets modelled by Christ in creating an intimate cell of followers, but it's also young people, in general, who are creating and being drawn to these groups. As an article in *Christianity Today* revealed, these communities 'attract mostly twenty-somethings who long for community, intimacy with Jesus, and to love those on the margins of society. And they are willing to give up the privileges to which they were born.'[11]

'Intimate community' has been a buzz phrase amongst Gen X churchgoers for years, and growing numbers of Gen Xers and younger generations appear to be revolting against churches that offer a comfortable, middle-class version of faith. This 'new' type of church offers a clear and gospel-motivated alternative to consumer culture. It has also found, much like the church of the New Testament and the campaigns of Wesley and Whitefield, that where the gospel most appeals to the masses is amongst the marginalized.

Can the church compete?

Within a deeply materialistic society, perhaps it's churches offering a 'new monasticism' that will provide a vision that's radical enough to entice young people away from consumer lifestyles. In a culture where young people have their appetites for distraction permanently sated, it's becoming increasingly difficult to communicate the unique appeal of the gospel. As a recent Navigator survey of spirituality amongst young Europeans discovered, most young people judge spirituality on the basis of the question, 'What's in it for me?' So what's the 'brand' appeal of Christianity? How does it stand out from the crowd? How can the church compete with the non-stop milieu of soaps, celebs, drugs, sex and MTV?

As writer Neil Postman concluded, society's drive to create entertainment media with an increasing ability to captivate people's attention isn't going to go away. We're becoming increasingly adept at creating fake worlds that are even better than the real thing. It's a world where Aldous Huxley's version of the future in *A Brave New World* has come true, and not George Orwell's bleak, totalitarian view of Britain in *1984*. Huxley foresaw a society that never objected to oppression by brutal regimes because they were too captivated by their material advantages – the truth had been lost in trivia.[12]

Certainly today, the role of religion in young people's lives has been trivialized. There *are* far better versions of reality on offer, as the tragic case of one Chinese teen recently proved. She was so immersed in an online role-playing computer game that took place over several days that she hadn't stopped to break for enough sleep or food.

A recent research project on spirituality conducted specifically amongst Britain's young people indicated that religion and spiritual matters hardly register a flicker on young people's radar. In their book *Ambiguous Evangelism*, Bob Mayo, Sara Savage and Sylvie Collins discuss the challenges faced in trying to engage people with matters of faith in contemporary society. Savage refers to French writer Daniele Hervieu-Leger in order to define the process of secularization:

> [Hervieu-Leger] describes secularization as a loss of religious memory, by which she means there has been a loss of the particular way of believing and practising Christianity, which included legitimization of the faith by the authority of the

> Church and the passing on of a tradition from one generation to another down a lineage of believers.[13]

God and the church are rapidly fading aspects of cultural memory, so there are fewer and fewer wider social structures or stories that lend credence to or legitimize religion. Our media rarely seek actively to create positive associations with Christianity or any other faith. And although our schools have become more sensitive to observing various religious festivals and some form of religious education is carried out in most schools, the approach has more to do with promoting tolerance and citizenship than with seriously discussing the validity of each faith's core beliefs. The impact of this can be to trivialize the role of religion, as Savage highlights with an insightful quote from Cox and Cairns, who write:

> Failing to take into account the truth claims of religions has two consequences. Practically it means that the teaching is confined to the externals of religions, their places of worship, their cult objects and their festivals. Their deeper beliefs which justify those places, objects and festivals are carefully avoided in case they raise truth claims. Such teaching can give the impression that religion is a superficial set of customs practised by those who happen to like them. More profoundly the avoidance of truth claims can suggest that no type of religion can have any deep significance, nor lead to truth, and therefore that religious education is not an imperative study, and can be indoctrination into agnosticism.[14]

Because there isn't a popular voice that legitimizes faith, the role of communities represented by the new monasticism, in taking a stand against societal norms, could be lending much needed authenticity to the church's truth claims. It's very hard to argue with the impact that communities such as Manchester's Eden Project have had when crime figures have been on a downward trend in the area since the community's inception.

New mission fields?

As I'll examine in a case study shortly, when it comes to creating disciples, making headway with young people who have had little or no previous contact with church often comes at the cost of great personal sacrifice for individuals and church communities alike. The parallels are there again with 'mission' abroad. It's the youth workers who involve themselves with the culture, who go where young people go, who celebrate how they celebrate, be it at a McDonalds or a nightclub, and who invest time and energy in developing relationships. But we fool ourselves if we think that those youth workers can then extract new disciples from those contexts and put them in mainstream churches without extensive 'reorientation' – and that doesn't mean simply putting them on an Alpha course.

It's often the youth workers who are part of experimental churches who can most readily create spaces for exploration and worship that are, in effect, 'stepping stones'. These spaces sit in between the peer group context in which young people find themselves and the existing faith community. One way of making headway with young people in terms of introducing them to faith is through offering them a communal or peer context that holds more significance for them than the one in which they already find themselves.

'Romance Academy' is one such illustration of how this works. The project began when two youth workers in north London, Dan Burke and my wife Rachel Gardner, were approached by a media company who wanted to document their attempts to teach teens the value of taking a fresh look at sexual relationships. The result was the Romance Academy. Twelve teens from a variety of social, ethnic and religious backgrounds took a pledge to abstain from sex for five months, meeting week by week to hear ideas on the value of sex and relationships from Dan and Rachel, but also to discuss and critique their own and their peers' approach to relationships.

Although there was only one Christian in the group at the start, after the project finished one teen had undergone a strong experience of God and two others have recently been baptized. The Bible wasn't mentioned at all during fifteen weeks of meetings, nor were there any attempts at direct evangelism, so how did this happen?

There were several elements that led the young people to 'consider' becoming Christians. First there was the dedication of Dan and Rachel as youth workers, willingly becoming taxis for the teenagers, helping them fill out housing benefit forms, inviting them round for meals, and so on.

Then there was the X factor. Although Rachel and Dan didn't mention faith when it came to teaching the value of abstaining from sexual relationships, they were obviously teaching Christian values. And when the group began to experience the benefit of living a life where sex had more value than it had previously, they naturally associated it with Rachel's and Dan's 'different' way of life.

Much has been said about wisdom being the new evangelism, but here it worked. A sexually abstinent lifestyle began to make sense to young people in terms of how they saw themselves and others. One young woman summed it up as no longer wanting to give up her 'dignity' for casual sex. Importantly, though, the wisdom wasn't simply passed down from Dan and Rachel. It also evolved from discussions in the group. This meant that the new wisdom had automatic peer approval, because these views weren't developed in isolation. Many of the positive outcomes of the group came from a cocktail of both passed-down and peer-generated wisdom.

Romance Academy also helped introduce young people to the concept of faith – no mean feat. Many youth evangelists are faced with the task of trying to introduce faith to a generation for whom spirituality has little significance. Spirituality and the big questions of life rarely interrupt the daily bustle of texting, music, Playstation, drinking, sex, drug taking and channel surfing. And although young people may face issues of alienation and angst, they in no way perceive that spirituality might offer an answer to some of their dilemmas. As one youth evangelist put it, young people today are spiritually dehydrated rather than spiritually thirsty. If you're just thirsty, you know that what will satisfy you is water. If you're dehydrated, you may get symptoms such as headaches, but you may not realize that the cause was simply failing to drink enough water.

Romance Academy, if you like, alerted those young people to their condition. In a society where there's little space for reflection, twelve young people took time out and as a result started thinking differently about life. This was because they knew Dan and Rachel are Christians, but also because the issue of sex – something that's a big blip on their radar – was being addressed. Encouraging them to analyse and reflect on their own values, their peers' values and society's values opened them up to asking other big questions.

You could say that it was a blue pill/red pill *Matrix* moment. Romance Academy invited them to see an alternative to the 'truth' with which society presented them, and although that alternative truth was difficult to live out, they preferred it to 'having the wool pulled over their eyes'.

In a sense, what happened with Romance Academy is similar to what happened in the early church with catechesis. Catechesis originally meant oral instruction, but came to mean simply religious instruction. As Martyn Atkins, principal of Cliff College, outlined at a recent LICC conference, catechesis was a vital part of introducing pagans to the Christian faith. People often came to faith by asking people who were 'followers of the way' how they could find out more. In an age when Christianity was heavily persecuted, the first step would be to introduce them to a small cell of believers – they didn't want to risk leading Roman informants straight to the whole congregation. In this small cell the emphasis at first wouldn't be so much on instructing people in the beliefs of Christianity, but rather on extracting the old values of the pagan way of life. It was a breaking down in order to build up.

In a relatively gentle way, Romance Academy did the same thing, albeit by focusing on one particular area of life, namely sex. It's a valuable lesson. What we need are not more introductions to Christianity, but introductions to faith full stop. To an extent, Romance Academy fits this bill and does it in a way that appeals to young people. Are you going to get teenagers automatically interested in a course that aims to debunk and dissect the values of pop culture from a Christian perspective? Not always. Are you more likely to get them to talk about sex . . . ?

This isn't about sowing seeds, it's about breaking up the ground before you can sow the seed. As one youth mission study put it, what we need is 'prior mission'.

> Prior mission is about encouraging imagination, going beyond clichéd symbols . . . and allowing young people to articulate their own questions. Prior mission starts with the reality of who young people are, and the questions they are asking. This will involve a primary focus on who young people want to become rather than what young people should be doing.[15]

Again the church needs to realize exactly how much of a mission context it finds itself in when trying to reach young people, so that it can produce culturally appropriate methods of introducing the concept of faith in Christ.

Ambiguous Evangelism points out just how hard the ground is that we need to break up. For example, we may try to create bridges between secular and Christian culture by using video games, songs, films and TV programmes that make references to religion, be it *Bruce Almighty* or *The Chronicles of Narnia*. But although we as believers may make the connection, young people don't readily invest it with religious significance in any shape or form. So 'Angel' is a song sung by Robbie Williams, end of story. Even though we may painstakingly outline the concept of having a guardian angel watching over you and how that refers back to incidents in the Bible, it would take a serious amount of time and energy to establish the example as anything other than a momentary part of the ebb and flow of media montage that makes up youth culture today.

There's simply no wider frame of reference to connect these ideas to the concepts that would make them significant. Many teen males wanted to see *The Passion of the Christ* because of its status as a modern-day 'video nasty', not because it was a biopic of the most influential religious figure in history.

So what frame of reference do young people use? We've uncovered a good deal of what matters to young people in terms of image, consumerism and peer affiliations. The authors of *Ambiguous Evangelism* (Mayo, Savage and Collins) have come up with a phrase that, although not exactly catchy, sums up young people's worldview and how they relate to 'spirituality' – 'happy midi-narrative'.

> The term midi-narrative was used in order to distinguish it from the idea of meta-narrative. Whereas a meta-narrative suggests a teleological influence – a universal truth that makes sense of life as an unfolding story on a grand scale (as in Marxism, Enlightenment 'progress' or Judaeo-Christian end times) – the world view of young people is on the more modest scale of life here and now, rather than something from beyond. However it is not purely individualistic (mini), but communal. Hence, the prefix 'midi' is an attempt to indicate the scope of the story-line.[16]

'Happy' therefore refers generally to the state of young people's emotional well-being, but also describes their goal. In their communal story, 'happiness' within the peer group is paramount.

As the study by Mayo, Savage and Collins revealed, there's little sense that religion plays a major part in young people's lives. Rather, they identified a shared story born of materialism:

> The study identified a coherent narrative, which could be encapsulated as: this world and all life in it, is meaningful as it is; there is no need to think of significance as somewhere else. Implicit in this world view . . . is the view that the universe and the social world are essentially benign. Although

> difficult things do happen in life, there are enough resources within the individual and their family and friends to enable happiness to prevail. Happiness is the goal of life. As one young person said 'happiness is the ideal you aim for . . .'[17]

We could only have arrived at this perspective on life, the universe and everything within the confines of the latter half of the twentieth century and the start of the twenty-first. Never have we been better able to satisfy our endless appetite for distraction. 'Good Times' is the theme tune for the post-war generations. As Bob Mayo comments, whether 'good times' means clubbing or playing computer games:

> . . . as the *Evening Standard* put it, having it all is seen as a right not a luxury. One of the findings of the research, therefore, was that people feel generally happy and are not feeling the lack of religion; people don't miss what they don't know.[18]

Conclusions

What does this mean in terms of reaching today's generations? As a generation that lives for experience, they need to 'experience' an alternative lifestyle that's better than the one they've already got. Can we appeal to felt psychological needs in order to fill people's 'God-shaped' vacuum if that vacuum is no longer experienced, if life itself has too much to offer people? And even though we may perceive life 'in secular society' to be a roller-coaster ride of emotional highs and extreme lows, there's always the next party / drug / video game / movie / concert to pick you up again. The 'happy midi-narrative' dominates.

As technology advances, entertainment's ability to attract and distract is only going to get better. The likes of film directors Steven Spielberg and George Lucas are already researching 3D movies that let you live inside the movie, and the same is planned for video games. (Incidentally, video games made $9.9 billion in the US in 2005, while the US cinema box office took $9.4 billion.)

So how do we appeal to today's generations? Much has been said of the Gen Xers' desire for intimate community, and this is obviously echoed by the communities of the 'new monasticism'. If today's young people find happiness through relationships with peers and through peer acceptance, then offering them a more significant edge to those relationships is one way forward. It's how Romance Academy worked, and it's why youth cells in church are so popular.

It was C. S. Lewis who said that as humans we're 'too easily pleased'. Our prospect as church is to create communities where simple 'happiness' isn't good enough, where we yearn to make deep connections with both Creator and created, where we're willing to explore what it means to be made in God's image through imitating Christ.

Notes

1. D. Buckingham, *After the Death of Childhood*, pp. 50–51.
2. R. Bell, *Velvet Elvis*, p. 81.
3. Head to www.licc.org.uk/imagine for more information.
4. T. Sine, *Mustard Seed Versus McWorld*, p. 221.
5. C. Lasch, *The Culture of Narcissism*, p. 7.
6. M. Wroe (ed.), *God: What the Critics Say*, p. 16.
7. B. Mayo *et al.*, *Ambiguous Evangelism*, p. 29.
8. G. Tomlin, *The Provocative Church*, p. 54.
9. T. Wright, *Luke for Everyone*, p. 184.
10. Tomlin, *The Provocative Church*, pp. 64–65.
11. *Christianity Today*, September 2005.
12. N. Postman, *Amusing Ourselves to Death*, pp. vii–viii.

13. Mayo *et al.*, *Ambiguous Evangelism*, p. 13.
14. Ibid., p. 23.
15. S. Savage *et al.*, *Making Sense of Generation Y*, p. 121.
16. Mayo *et al.*, *Ambiguous Evangelism*, p. 144.
17. Ibid., p. 34.
18. Ibid., p. 35.

PART 3

MEND THE GAP: BEING GOD'S KINGDOM COMMUNITY

8. GENERATIONAL TENSIONS: CAN THE GAP BE BRIDGED?

A tradition can only progress when it encounters strife or challenges from the inside and the outside.
(Alisdair Macintyre)[1]

It's all that the young can do for the old, to shock them and keep them up to date.
(George Bernard Shaw)

Generation X – the 'bridge' generation

Many books, such as *God and the Generations*, have outlined the difference between generational strands in today's world. The world is split into 'the Builder Generation' – those born between 1925 and 1945; 'the Boomer Generation' – born between 1946 and 1963; 'Generation X' – born between 1964 and 1981; and last but not least, 'Generation Y', also known as the 'Millennial Generation', born from 1982 onwards.[2] While there are marked differences in attitudes between each strand, there also seems to be a more distinct division between those born before and after the early 1960s.

Do we then have to accept that Generation X and subsequent generations operate within a frame of reference that ultimately does separate them from the more 'mature' Boomer and Builder generations? Gen X, after all, is the first generation to experience media saturation in every area of life. For Generations X and Y, our common binding story becomes that of TV and pop culture – for instance, the latest celebrated comedy turn that infects language in the playground, the office and the staff room. This is a factor that

David Walliams and Matt Lucas understood in investing *Little Britain* with a catchphrase for every character.

Perhaps it's due to the arrival of perpetual adolescence in culture (we extend notions of play into adulthood; we suspend 'responsibility' for longer), but today's thirty-somethings frequently celebrate the same cultural icons as late teenagers. If you loved alt rock band (grunge) Nirvana in the 1990s, you'll love Nine Black Alps today. And if you're a late teen who missed seminal indie band The Pixies the first time round in the late 1980s, then you can catch them on their reform tour and marvel at how many bands they've influenced. And there are many 34-year-olds who'd give 15-year-olds a run for their money on any video game they care to name. I recently attended a Franz Ferdinand gig, and the audience was predominantly a mix of thirty-somethings right down to late teens.

Is this why most youth workers tend to be from Gen X or Y? Do we unconsciously acknowledge a distinct generational boundary between Boomers and Gen Xers already in the church? It's either the case that we believe Gen X and Y to be best suited for the job as they 'speak the lingo', or it's the case that Boomers are simply put off by their perceptions of youth culture and feel they can't relate. But again, if this is the case, why haven't we factored it into our leadership of the church? If youth are the church of tomorrow today, why aren't we more adventurous in how we adapt church for their expectations?

When faced with the challenges of attracting new generations to Christ, it's obvious that we do have to discern whether rifts between generations in the church are insurmountable. We have to discern whether or not the generations who are predominantly in charge of churches, denominations and parachurch mission organizations are (without the overt influence of newly emergent generations) the ones best equipped to encourage young people to become part of authentic Christian communities. Are they capable of teaching young people that in today's society we have to earn our right to proclaim the truth by living it first?

The clashes that have marked differing generational expectations have been commented on *ad infinitum* since the birth of youth culture. The problem is that these clashes are still evident – in the widely different approaches to teaching, worship, evangelism, the use of church buildings, even the need for church buildings. Do we have to admit that we've reached stalemate? Is that why many Gen Xers are desperate to experiment with new concepts of church?

We're back to the new wine question, back to the problem of 'generational myopia'. As the old Chinese proverb says, if you want to ask what water is like, don't ask a fish. Is it the case that the generations in charge of the church are trapped in an operational worldview that simply can't discern how, when and most particularly why change needs to take place in terms of how we 'do' and 'become' church? It's obviously not deliberate, but in terms of reaching today's generations, current leaders of church and parachurch organizations are short sighted – that is, they have 'generational myopia'.

One example of this generational myopia is the way the church approaches the problem of the generation gap and reaching out to youth culture. In essence, the church has provided a short-term solution for what's really a long-term problem. The problem is a breakdown in communication between old and young generations. The answer the church has found is not to equip the older generation to relate better to the younger, but to appoint someone else to do it on their behalf.

Let me expand. As previous chapters have pointed out, youth culture is seen as being alien to adult norms. As a result, in reaching out to an 'alien' culture, the church has often adopted an overseas mission mentality when it comes to youth work: employ a specialist who speaks the lingo, so that you don't have to, and who will conduct a mission that doesn't directly impact *your* church. That specialist is the youth worker.

So what impact does this have on trying to bridge the generational gap?

To continue with the overseas mission analogy, we wouldn't expect a missionary in China to transplant their congregation successfully into our own without making big changes to church structure. Similarly, we can't expect a youth worker to integrate youth work successfully with mainstream church without adapting church structure. Yet for some reason we rarely see the necessity for radical change in the church.

Many churches will appoint a youth worker and say, 'Do what it takes to reach young people.' Many denominations or parachurch organizations will appoint a youth specialist and give them *carte blanche* to reach a specific niche group. But is this enough? It seems to be the case that churches and organizations will always stop short of handing over the reins of leadership to younger generations – a move that would surely broaden the organization's vision and perspective. It seems that young generations are only ever given authority to *reach* young generations, and rarely to adapt church so that everybody can reach each other. Generation X, although best equipped to lead the church, is often simply sidelined into leading youth work.

This is why the number one problem faced by youth workers is one of integration. Youth workers are great at reaching young people, but what do they do with them once they've reached them? Ask a detached youth worker or a schools worker to which local church they'd send the kids they reach on a Sunday morning, and they may struggle to reply.

So we have to ask this question: in creating and supporting the role of youth workers, has the church been short sighted?

Generational myopia

It's also worth asking at this point, what really needs to change? Do churches need to become more 'relevant' in order to embrace young people who come through their doors on Sunday? Or do we need to change the expectations of the young people who enter church on a Sunday morning? Should we present them with some form of discipleship programme or catechesis that educates young people about their role in joining a church community?

This latter approach is certainly part of the solution, but what we desperately need to address is the issue of church structure and generational myopia. Graham Cray, bishop of Maidstone and youth culture commentator, stated in a recent lecture that structural change within churches and parachurch organizations is often difficult to facilitate because of certain characteristics of the generations who typically run them.

Typically, the leaders are Baby Boomers, born after World War II, and they're the type of people who understand that running the church and getting on with things is just something their generation has always done – so why not continue to lead? Also, due to better healthcare, people in such positions have found that they can remain active for longer. They effectively make a retirement career out of running the church. And members of this generation are often of the opinion that there are relatively few people to whom they can pass the baton – at least, few people who would maintain the church or organization in a way they'd approve.

You may think this summary is accurate, or you may think it's harsh, and how you view it may depend on your age! But think of the role of the youth worker in a church – it's a role that's rarely equated with serious church leadership, and a glance at the difference in salaries between senior church leaders and youth workers would prove the point. It has often been said that youth work is seen as a 'stepping stone' career on the way to 'senior' church leadership. Doesn't that say a great deal about the perceived role of youth work in the church? It's apparently more about simply 'holding on' to younger generations, than about equipping them for active leadership.

Unconsciously or otherwise, the church may have swallowed whole the media panics about the state of youth in our country, and so may be reluctant to let them 'inherit'. As psychologist Christine Griffin points out, in today's world, 'dominant constructions of youth serve to link young people with "specific" social problems solely or primarily as a consequence of their youth'.[3]

With so many negative connotations attached to 'youth culture', it's no wonder that older generations are reluctant to hand over the leadership of the church. So what's the diagnosis? What's the cure? Do we need a switch in leadership? Does Generation X need to be in charge of the church in order for it to move forward? There has been plenty of analysis of the problem over recent years. Much has been written on how to reach Gen X or Gen Y, and there have been endless seminars on creating emerging churches that are culturally relevant for a changing world. To an extent, however, these have only encouraged the overseas mission mentality – that the church needs specialists to do the job, people who understand the culture. What we haven't truly convinced ourselves is that *all* churches are in a fresh mission context, like it or not. We're already in the field, and so – to employ a crude battle metaphor – those specialists should be at the head of the charge and not sent out like lone snipers.

Is the problem that the people in charge of the church are like doctors operating in the nineteenth century – great at what they do, perfectly knowledgable, but without a contemporary approach to the problem that will result in the best cure? Re-educating such leaders would take up too much time and too many resources, and the need is too urgent. We need to search for a more immediate and longer lasting solution.

Perhaps it's time to come to the realization that as a church we simply can't recover. The damage has been done. We can either expend a great deal of energy trying to 'remarry' the different age groups, or we can, effectively, rip it up and start again – new wine for new wineskins.

Meeting generational expectations

If that prospect seems too gloomy, then perhaps now is the time to proffer one possible solution. The following quote is from Cam Marston, a business guru whose approach encourages businesses to see the advantages that 'cross-generational' co-operation can afford:

> For the first time in history, four distinct generations – Matures, Boomers, Xers and Millenials – are employed side by side in the workplace. With differing values and seemingly incompatible views on leadership, these generations have

> stirred up unprecedented conflict in the business world. Effective management of this generational divide is vital to longevity and success. In fact it is the most important demand your company can make of its leaders.[4]

Substitute 'workplace' and 'business' for 'church', and you've got a fairly accurate summary of the state of Christianity in the twenty-first century and a pointer to how crucial it is for churches to acknowledge that the needs of different generations need to be represented in all aspects of leadership. This is a unique time in history: never before have such distinct generations operated side by side in the church. Unfortunately, the 'unique' response of the church to the problem, that is, youth work, is not a long-term answer to the problem of generational divide.

So why not take bold steps when it comes to appointing leaders for the boards of our churches and parachurch organizations? Ask yourself if there are any members of Gen X or Gen Y on the board of your church or organization, and if there are, are they lone voices? Radically different times call for a radical vision. But if this isn't the message we want to hear, expect more and more generational splits within the church – youth workers who work with Gen Y leaving churches to form their own communities, and as a result siphoning off young people from other churches as well.

Of course there are always exceptions to the rules. Just as we shouldn't write off young generations for being 'immature', we shouldn't assume that older generations lack vision. A number of Anglican bishops have been foresighted enough to encourage and initiate experimental churches, even if those experimentations fail to some degree, as with the infamous 'Nine O'Clock' service in Sheffield in the 1990s.

But is it happening often enough and fast enough? You can't help but think that if there were bishops from Generation X, it would create a new atmosphere of experimentation and exchange. Is that so unrealistic? In Surrey in 2005, a 20-year-old was appointed as a justice of the peace. That person's suitability for the role was questioned, largely on the grounds of lack of experience. But if we don't take risks, how will we know, how will we learn?

What the church needs is not more youth advisors, but more young leaders. Recent figures show that the average age of people training for ordination in the Anglican Church is 44.

Perhaps we need to understand that our youth workers aren't youth workers at all. They're church leaders who work with young people, the church and the wider community. If we see the role of youth worker in our church as subordinate to the role of senior pastor, then it seems that we're guilty of viewing children and youth as 'becomings' and not 'beings' in their own right.

We have to assess realistically whether or not the generation who currently dominate as leaders of the church are unintentionally but nevertheless effectively bridling growth. Attempting to create change in the church at the moment can seem like trying to turn round an oil tanker.

Generation X – a difficult child

This isn't to say, however, that handing over the reins to Generation X really is the solution. It's not exactly like swapping an oil tanker for a speedboat. Generation X may have more openness to change and new cultural forms, but in one sense Generation X has had a problematic childhood in the church.

Whereas Generation Y has relatively little or no understanding of religion or church, Gen X grew up with enough knowledge of church to want to reject it. If you like, Gen X is the teenager of church culture. Just as the dominant language of the teenager is rebellion against adult norms, so many Gen X forms of church can be seen partly as rebellion against 'traditional' church.

In effect, Gen X is first-generation technology: any new technology will have bugs that need to be worked out of the system. Gen X is the first generation to be ushered into the multimedia age, so its responses to church will be born of a need to innovate and create, but will also be born of frustration.

One of the forms of church clearly associated with Gen X is 'alternative' worship. As singer/songwriter Tom Waits said when picking up an award for alternative music at a highly esteemed ceremony in America, 'Alternative to what?' When it comes to alt worship, it has meant doing things differently from mainstream church – not necessarily as an attempt to find culturally 'cool' forms of worship, but more to find styles of worship that express meaning for their generation. This isn't to say that all Gen X church attendees find alt worship to be the most appropriate way of celebrating faith. As *God and the Generations* surmised, the members of a particular generation group, be it Xers or Boomers, don't all respond in the same way:

> People of the same age group may live through the same historical events in the same country, and yet interpret those events in quite different ways according to the social generational unit to which they belong . . . so not all Generation X are cynical slackers, some are IT entrepreneurs and CEO's, others are evangelists.[5]

Many Gen Xers are perfectly happy with church the way it is.

Bringing change to the church isn't about seeking out new and experimental ideas simply for the sake of change. It's about taking a more active role in determining the needs and expectations not simply of 'youth', but of the various generations who find themselves jockeying for position in the body of the church.

Take Generation Y as another example, those born post-1980. The style of church that has most appealed to this generation in the UK is undoubtedly Soul Survivor. In terms of worship style, Soul Survivor isn't so different from the style initiated by Graham Kendrick – one man with a guitar leading a band with backing singers. Worship leaders like Matt Redman simply provided young people with their own tried and tested format that they could utilize for themselves. It's a style that has come to dominate 'youth' worship to the extent that today's youth groups rarely experiment with other worship expressions. So once again it's not necessarily the case that younger generations' designs for church always mean finding novel ideas week in, week out.

Testing reflexes

Is there, however, any way we can find a 'one-size-fits-all' style of church? In discussions revolving around emerging or contemporary church, it's a common thread that 'models' can't be trusted. Simple analysis of the needs of different generations won't automatically generate an understanding of a one-size-fits-all cure.

There's obviously no quick fix. So we make a mistake if we think media-saturated generations will only respond to multisensory, multimedia churches. Just because young people have been presented with a world dominated by information technology and consumerism doesn't mean that this world provides for all their needs.

In a world where, as ex-presidential candidate Al Gore puts it, 'genuine political dialogue has been almost completely replaced by high stakes competition for the ever shortening attention span of the electorate', we need to approach contemporary culture with a critical attitude. Older generations can help to encourage this. They shouldn't shrink from their role as wisdom givers, but should embrace it all the more, and teaching in the church should empower them for that role. More of that in the next chapter.

So where does this leave the church? In seeking to respond to huge cultural fluxes, we have to understand that at the heart of such changes are increasing contrasts between frames of reference for differing generations. This is outlined in the way different churches have responded to cultural change – in some contexts trying to find new language, new expressions, in others trying to preserve existing language and tradition. What we see within present church culture are three main reactions to generational divide: resistance, compromise and experiment.

Resistance

These churches may be dominated by mature generations, or Boomers, and are resistant to changing the form or function of church in order to fit in with the current cultural climate. This is either through a lack of will or lack of know-how.

Compromise

This can happen on a small or large scale. For many churches, compromise means 'doing something for the young people' – for example, a family service once a month.

This compromise often involves merely creating separate spaces in which young people can express themselves with little adult input other than the youth work team, and it rarely affects mainstream church. What happens on Friday night has little impact on Sunday mornings.

Then there are churches that embrace niche groups on different levels. For example, an inner-city Anglican church may conduct an 8 a.m. traditional service mainly attended by matures, an 11 a.m. service aimed at families and a 7 p.m. service which is attended by twenty- and thirty-somethings. It's a bit like a 'website' church: there's one homepage with various sections that correlate and overlap.

Some may criticize such churches for failing to unite the generational strands and may feel that the church is simply acting as a 'service' provider, tailoring to the needs of individual groups. A more accurate summary would be that these churches are simply providing a coherent response to 'generational' tensions. You can't please all the people all the time, so why not have a variety of 'congregations' under one roof rather than having to provide separate buildings, resources and workers for them all?

The fact that differing age groups prefer different services just serves to highlight generational distinctions. Obviously no one form of service can really be determined as more valid than any other, so preference for a traditional service over an alternative worship format is tied to issues of taste rather than disagreement over doctrine. There are relatively few contemporary protests that the organ is a more sacred instrument than an acoustic guitar or DJ decks.

Experiment

This covers a whole range of responses from 'emerging' church through to intergenerational worship. A church may not choose to create 'niche' congregations (that is, with divisions between adult and youth), but may mix up teaching and worship styles – for example, meditations set to music and traditional expositional preaching one week, and the next week group-led choruses and an artistic, involved congregational response to a biblical theme.

Also, as niche congregations in themselves are experimental, this may mean creating a mono-generational church or a congregation defined by social context. So a church may be made up largely of teenagers, churched or unchurched, or, alternatively, thirty-somethings. A detached youth work reaching out to young people on an estate may start as a cell group, may then grow into a mono-generational youth church, but may evolve further to include different ages over time.

Conclusion

Part of the response to generational tensions within the church should obviously be ongoing dialogue between those generations. As you've probably gathered from this chapter, I believe that such a discussion should be 'chaired' by members of Generation X. They provide a unique perspective as the bridge generation. They need to listen to the wisdom of the mature generations and respect the passions of Generation Y. If these voices aren't heard, the tensions will never be resolved.

We also need to rethink seriously the role of youth work. The various approaches to church currently employed do indicate a felt need to respond to the challenges of living in today's world, the challenge of reaching today's generations. But by and large, the greatest response to the challenge is still to employ a youth worker in order to reach the young. Youth workers do amazing work and their role is key to church survival, but if it's our only solution, it's a superficial response considering the extent of the dilemma we face.

For many churches, though, employing a youth worker does appear to be a response that has a positive impact on the growth of their church. As an article in *Christianity* magazine pointed out, churches that employ youth workers – be it on a part- or full-time basis – experience growth, while those that don't, don't.[6] It's hard to say, of course, whether this is genuine growth or migratory growth: parents with young or teenage children are more likely to attend a church that provides more services for young people, even if it means commuting.

However, the increasing need for qualified youth workers brings other issues to bear. Most theology and youth work courses offer secular accreditation such as a JNC certificate (Joint Negotiating Committee for Youth and Community Workers). This means that graduates can choose careers in the church or in secular organizations, and there are no prizes for guessing which context offers fewer working hours for, in many cases, nearly twice as much pay.

So is youth work in its current form ultimately part of the problem, or part of the solution? The question the church has been asking for the last forty years, in response to the growth of youth culture, is this: how do we reach and keep young people? The answer has been the youth worker. I believe, however, that the question needs to be expanded, even rephrased. For the future of the church, we need to discern three things: What does it mean to be an adult in today's world? What does it mean to be a disciple? What does it mean to be family?

Notes

1. T. Beaudoin, *Virtual Faith*, p. 152.
2. D. Hilborn and M. Bird (eds), *God and the Generations*.
3. C. Griffin, 'Representations of the Young', in J. Roche and S. Tucker (eds), *Youth in Society*, p. 21.
4. Information taken from www.cammarston.com.
5. Hilborn and Bird (eds), *God and the Generations*, pp. 96–97.
6. *Christianity*, September 2003.

9. A FAMILY AFFAIR

> Is it possible that the 'problem' facing youth ministry reflects all too accurately a malaise infecting mainline denominations generally: a flabby theological identity due to an absence of passion? That would be ironic, most young people come to us brimming with passion. Could it be that instead of fanning this youthful zeal into holy fire, we have more often doused it, dismissed it, or drowned it in committee meetings?
> (Kenda Creasy Dean)[1]

It wasn't the answer the youth worker expected. When she asked the two teenage girls what they thought was lacking in their church, she thought they'd list the usual suspects: not enough teenage boys, no alternative rock music, not enough chance for them to have their say. What they said, though, was 'respect for God'. They thought the church lacked reverence – and this from teenagers whose families don't attend church.

What teenagers look for in church is a tangible fervour for God. Kenda Creasy Dean is right in surmising that we don't make enough of the passion of youth. This is largely because as adults we've often failed to build churches that revel in Christ's promise of giving life and life to the full. We've modelled churches that are far too often tied to dogma and bureaucracy, churches that expend too much energy in maintaining outmoded ideas of what it means to be church.

As a result, many of the 'churched' youth who enter adolescence don't always bring with them a verve for their faith. They may enjoy the special youth events, the energy and enthusiasm of a big worship event at a Christian festival, but are they dedicated to growing personally in their love and knowledge of God? As most church youth groups grow through contagion – teens passionate for Christ bringing along non-Christian friends to church – the state of our young people's faith is of primary concern in terms of growing church communities.

Adults modelling passionate faith is the solution not just to bridging the generation gap, but also to creating young disciples who will maintain a love for their faith through childhood, teenage years and beyond. It's a solution that's at once simple and difficult – simple because it's so obvious; difficult because it seems to be something we find so hard to do. The priceless by-product of adults and young people sharing a passionate faith is that relationships between young and old remain healthy. As the teaching in both Old and New Testaments shows, a vibrant model of discipleship is one that actively seeks to nurture and maintain relationships at every level – with God, family, self, church, society and planet.

But what does a healthy young disciple look like? The team at LICC asked me to share my thoughts on what 'ingredients' made young people 'whole-life Christians' – people who passionately live out their faith in each and every context in which they find themselves. The following isn't a checklist, but it is something I'd use to direct the way we ensure that our young people have a robust faith.

In no particular order of importance, young 'whole-life' disciples would:

- grasp the different ways God reveals his nature: through Word, Spirit, people, creation and Jesus;
- understand Christ's mission in the light of God establishing his kingdom rule on earth;

- embrace the different genres used in the biblical narrative;
- come to understand that as God tells his story in different ways, so we express our worship of God through diverse means;
- acknowledge that just as Christ came to us as the living truth, the truth is something to which we bear witness in our lives through thought, word and action;
- have the tools to engage with the biblical narrative and develop an in-depth understanding of God's Word to us;
- know that the key to human flourishing is a life lived in intimate conversation with our heavenly Father;
- have a keen sense of the validity of their own story, in an age where a Christian worldview often seems out of step with the worldview presented by society at large;
- be active critics (not passive recipients) of the media, in a communications technology driven age;
- be able to assess confidently the effect of education to challenge or reinforce their faith;
- recognize their role in the church family – and their responsibility to respect adults, whilst acknowledging that adults must also respect them in terms of inviting them to participate;
- understand that every area of life is of interest to God and that their future career, be it as mother, priest, teacher or plumber, can be discerned as God's vocational calling;
- realize that God has given them talents he wants them to use for their enjoyment and for his glory, e.g. skills as footballers, musicians, artists, cooks, preachers, etc.;
- recognize that God has unique spiritual gifts for them that need to be identified and exercised.

To ensure that these areas are nurtured in young people, they first have to be nurtured in adults. We have to understand that we must embody the answers to the questions, 'What does it mean to be an adult?' and 'What does it mean to be a disciple in the twenty-first century?' Just as Christ didn't merely make statements about 'truth', but embodied truth as well, so we must embody Christian truth for our young people.

Strategic ideas for integration

How can we create a nurturing atmosphere? If we are to encourage our young people to be whole-life disciples, the church will need to be *intentional* in its focus. The following are concepts that I encourage churches to consider as they develop a plan for incorporating both young and old into their ministry. In the main these are ideas that aim to rebuild and strengthen foundations.

1. Make disciple-making the core story of our culture

Better strategies and better resources count for nothing if our core story or culture is not about disciple-making. It's a familiar saying in the business world that 'culture eats strategy for breakfast'. If we don't get the story at the heart of our community right, then all the programmes we run and all the resources we provide will only enable purely cosmetic changes. It takes a disciple to make a disciple. If the environment in which young people grow up is one of passionate discipleship, then they'll be passionate about being disciples.

2. Create positive rites of passage

Is there confusion over when childhood ends and when adulthood arrives? How does this impact child/adult relations?A good place to start thinking about integration is to challenge the way we view young people in the church. We could critique the ways young people create their own rites of passage, for example underage drinking, smoking and sex, but it's far better to create our own rituals that celebrate their coming of age.

3. Embrace a pioneering role – with humility

In seeking to unite differing generational strands, we're mapping new territory. It's important to bear in mind that no one has been here before. As we try to bring together generations with different cultural experiences and different expectations, we must have the humility to understand that we need God's wisdom and other people's experience. We need to listen to the 'journeys and stories' of the broader church in order to find ways forward.

4. Aim towards whole-life Christianity (and the destruction of the sacred/secular divide)

Celebrating the role of faith in church, at home, in our leisure time and in the workplace is vital if our young people are to grow up with the understanding that God is concerned with every area of our lives.

5. Work alongside the youth worker

What's the role of the youth worker – mission or maintenance? We shouldn't employ youth workers to 'manage' our young people, or to be 'surrogate spiritual parents' to our children. We need to be clear that they're there to assist and enable the rest of the congregation to raise children in the faith. And in terms of mission, the best missionaries to young people are young people themselves. The focus of a youth worker's ministry within the church should be as a teacher and facilitator – encouraging young people in the faith and providing opportunity for mission.

Enabling integration

These are broad concepts to bear in mind when thinking about integrating young people into church life, but how does this work out in reality? I still hold to point 3 above – that we're pioneering here – but the following puts some meat on the bones in terms of providing principles and practical ideas for creating integrated church. For resources connected to these strategies, including websites, books, media and training courses, see Appendix 2.

1. Restore confidence in our ability to pass down the faith

Like a great deal of things in life, our ability to pass on our faith successfully to young people depends on our confidence to do so. Our lack of ability to disciple young people stems from our lack of ability to disciple adults.

I dislike using 'marketplace' analogies, but here it's appropriate. Any salesperson can sell a product if they have confidence in it. Quality is easy to sell if it's priced right. If you're selling a car that does 500 miles to the gallon, has an onboard computer that makes crashes nigh impossible and the best safety record in the world, you wouldn't have a problem getting rid of a whole fleet of them.

You've probably guessed where I'm heading, but let's name that car 'Christianity'. Most adults in the church are happy to drive around in it, as long as they don't attract too much attention (maybe it's a nice metallic grey), but are blissfully unaware of all the car's finer features. When it comes to selling it, they have little confidence that anyone else would want to drive around in it. They're unaware of its safety record; they've never bothered to check how many miles to the gallon it does. And their 'mechanics' have never informed them properly, they've just told them how nice it is to drive around in one as well.

So how do we restore confidence in our product? We make everybody a mechanic as well as a driver. They don't have to be experts, they just need to know enough to have confidence in the quality of the car, its reliability, its potential. And do we need to attack our competitors? Does Rolls-Royce run advertising campaigns attacking 'lesser' brands? Who cares about the competitors when you have the best product going? The car sells itself.

In the marketplace of ideologies and beliefs, secular or religious, we have the best product out. The trouble is, we don't know it. Religious instruction in the church has fallen by the wayside, but before we discuss that further, here's a brief warning.

The other way to attempt to restore confidence is through church showmanship: we create big glitzy venues for our meetings, we have perfect worship teams, choirs, the works, wall-to-wall plasma screens and projector shows. We create a buzz that attracts hundreds, if not thousands. And in a sense churches that do this are redressing the balance. Church should be bold, exciting and energetic. Nonetheless, we have to be careful of creating just another communal peer adventure which people buy into but which has little intrinsic impact on lifestyle. It only maintains the appearance of success.

Going back to religious instruction, more and more churches are putting on evening classes or setting up theological centres, and why not? More and more people, especially those under 40, have been through further education. They're used to lecture-style learning as long as it's focused – that is, not 'thought for the day' sermons, but seminars on 'church history' or 'atonement', for example. Let's take advantage of that. Most of our pastors and church leaders who are equipped with theology degrees use precious little of what they've learnt in your average sermon, so why not put their skills to use? Shouldn't they also be teaching church history, missiology, doctrine, apologetics, communication skills?

In north Lancashire, the group of churches in which I grew up have done exactly this. They've provided a curriculum taught largely by the pastorate or lay members with specific training, and anyone can attend the Monday night sessions. It's a mix of lectures and interactive training, and my 21-year-old niece has just finished a preaching course which involved delivering a sermon to a group of pastors! She scored 82%, by the way.

Developing consistent adult education in the church is one way of restoring confidence. Making apologetics part of that education is key as well – on Sunday mornings and in house groups. A wealth of material on apologetics has been produced over recent years precisely because religious worldviews are being vigorously undermined, and churches need to make use of them (see Appendix 2). Some churches use the time dedicated to house or cell groups to put on teaching series. The groups meet together at the church and interact in those groups while listening to a specialist topic such as 'understanding Islam' for a set period of weeks.

Another way of restoring confidence is simply to stop spoon-feeding congregations. Sermons that require no response just encourage passivity. See Conrad Gempf's book *Jesus Asked* if you want to explore why asking and responding to questions was a vital part of Jesus' teaching method. He was continually forcing his disciples to think for themselves.

If we want our children to be wise in how they interact with the world, then we must have the wisdom to pass down in the first place. As I outlined in chapter 6, the passing on of wisdom was seen as a natural part of patriarchal responsibilities. Discipleship does begin at home. It's the duty of Christian parents and the wider congregation to try to impress a faith perspective on their children's outlook on life.

To achieve this we do need to restore Christians' confidence in their 'product'. We also need to assess whether or not we can, or indeed need to, reverse cultural trends that have impacted church and society and have resulted in the generation gap. We need to look at how the 'authority' of the family structure has been undermined and how we can passionately celebrate faith within the domestic context.

2. Emphasize the role of family as sacred community

An essential part of integrating young people into church is understanding just how much the church has unfortunately taken its cue from contemporary society, not the Bible, when it comes to being family and being community.

In chapter 6 I referred to Western culture becoming more 'kidicentric' – this is, family time becomes focused on entertaining children rather than on children assisting adults with their chores or joining in with adult activities.

Does this attitude transfer to church? Do children or adults drive the agenda for Sunday school? Is Sunday school focused on merely occupying the children while the adults 'do' church? Does it centre on entertainment and crafts because Sunday, after all, isn't about education but is part of our leisure time? Why can't the level to which we educate our young people about faith match the level they experience in education during the school week?

Further, would we need Sunday school at all if children were receiving sufficient education about their faith midweek? Would we need to split the church at all on a Sunday if we adopted Jesus' style of teaching? Presumably, when the disciples located the boy who had two loaves and fishes, they didn't find him in the Sunday school section of the crowd – something that Martin Wroe, Adrian Reith and Simon Parke echo in their book *101 Things Jesus Never Said*.

> Number 96
> 'OK OK – I'm twenty minutes into my parable now; so we'll have a silly kiddies song, and then could the Sunday school leave for their own activities? Because from here on in the words I use in the parable are going to be rather long, abstract and largely incomprehensible.'[2]

So what am I and others suggesting here? That we attempt to undo a hundred or so years of cultural constructs that revolve around 'childhood', 'adolescence' and 'youth culture'? That we fly in the face of twenty-first-century traditions which emphasize that the education of the young necessitates them being separated out into their own peer groupings?

Pretty much.

Isn't that what being part of a counterculture is all about? If society undervalues old age, then we check the biblical stream of teaching and find that old age is revered. So that's how the church should treat old people. If Jesus embraced children and gave them a vital place in the working out of his kingdom, that's what the church should do. If 12 years of age was old enough for Jesus to start sitting down with the elders of his faith to wrestle over biblical truth, that's what our 12-year-olds should be doing. And if both Old and New Testaments place high importance on parents instructing children in the faith, that's what we should be helping parents to do.

Our children are 'beings' in their own right, but – just like us – they're also 'becoming'. We're all realizing the potential God put in us when he made us in his own image; we're all becoming more like Christ. And part of that means that we associate 'growing up' not with becoming more independent, but with recognizing our 'co-dependence'.

It's an ideal that consultant paediatrician John Wyatt highlights when speaking against euthanasia and physician-assisted suicide. He speaks of the responsibilities of Christian communities in caring for the elderly, as well as medical communities providing better palliative care – not euthanasia – as an answer to people's suffering. The elderly depend on us as we once depended on them. God has built this co-dependence into our make-up. No mammal infant spends so long depending on its parents for survival as the human child. Dr Wyatt refers to this idea as 'mutual burdensomeness':

> I sometimes hear old people, including Christian old people who should know better, say, 'I'm happy to live my life as long as I can look after myself but I just don't want to be a burden to anyone else.'
>
> When you hear someone say that you must say, 'You're wrong. You are designed to be a burden. I am designed to be a burden to you and you are designed to be a burden to me.' We are meant to be a burden to one another. And the life of a family, including the life of the local church, the Christian family should be one of 'mutual burdensomeness'.[3]

He goes on to say:

> Here is an example where the authentic Christian community is going to become increasingly countercultural. In a culture which prizes independence we must model a way of community which demonstrates mutual burdensomeness. This is the way we are made, this is the way we are meant to live.[4]

In becoming incarnate, God wrote himself into this story of 'mutual burdensomeness'. God himself became a burden to an earthly mother, and even from the cross sought to ensure that his own mother would be taken care of.

As the core values of secular society drift further and further from any recognition of biblical mandates for communal living, the church needs to recognize where its own standards diverge and needs to fight to maintain them. The illustration of the frog in boiling water applies: chuck a frog into a pot of boiling water and it will jump out instantly; but place a frog into a pan of cold water and heat it slowly, and it won't respond to the temperature change, eventually dying.

When it comes to the church's attitude on youth, we desperately need to check the temperature. For instance, as I've already outlined, youth culture shouldn't really exist in a community that fully embraces biblical ideals. There should be no limbo between childhood and adulthood. But only when the church has redeemed biblical ideas of community and family life will it be able to heal the rifts that have formed between young and old.

We need to protect the sanctity of the family. We need to challenge aspects of contemporary life that undermine family life. We effectively need to eradicate the sacred/secular divide in the home. This doesn't mean swapping our kids' *Yu Gi Oh* DVDs for more *Veggie Tales*, but it does mean that we should recognize the family as a sacred community belonging to the 'priesthood of all believers'.

A family is church just as much as congregational meetings are on a Sunday. Church is a 24/7 vocation for old and young, but is this reflected in the way we celebrate faith in the home? Do we read the Bible to our children? Just as importantly, do our children see *us* reading the Bible on our own? Do we talk about faith at mealtimes, do we share quiet times and observe Christian festivals in a way that's truly meaningful?

A book called *Passing on the Faith* by Merton Strommen and Richard Hardel is an excellent place to start thinking through this issue. They quote Marjorie Thompson, who realizes that the church needs to review its vision of the family and challenge the sacred/secular divide:

> What if the family were not merely an object of the church's teaching mission, but one of the most basic units of the church's mission to the world? . . . what I am suggesting is that the communal church and the domestic church need to recapture a vision of the Christian family as a sacred community. This will require an awareness of the 'sacred' in the 'secular' – of God in the flesh of human life.[5]

Strommen and Hardel themselves make this clear in their mandate for the book: the church has to 'weed' out the influence of the sacred/secular divide on how we do/are church:

> Leaders recognise that in order to pass on the faith from generation to generation, a new paradigm of ministry is needed – one that is holistic and connects children, youth, family, congregation, community, and culture.

> The current paradigm has subtly conveyed the impression that faith is nurtured only in the church buildings. This has ultimately institutionalised the faith, a phenomenon found in both the Roman Catholic and Protestant churches.[6]

So how can we accomplish this? How can we support parents in their role as 'wisdom givers' to the next generation? As well as encouraging more adult training in the church, we also need specifically to assist parents in their responsibilities.

3. Train parents

Many churches are now running parenting courses. It only takes a cursory look at the TV programme *Supernanny* to realize that many modern parents feel out of their depth when it comes to setting helpful boundaries for their children without stifling their creativity. But as 'Supernanny' told one tearful mum, 'If there's no discipline in this house, how are you going to teach them right from wrong?'

Earlier I discussed how often domestic agendas revolve around the needs and wants of children. Adults fit their time round what children want to do, not vice versa. So when it comes to passing down the faith, it becomes difficult to fit such education into a child's timetable. In the strong patriarchal setting of many Muslim communities, the child rarely questions the instructions of an adult, so it's no surprise that many Muslim children can commit to hours of Koran reading each night.

I'm not suggesting a return to Victorian discipline and an approach to biblical teaching that's tantamount to indoctrination. There is, though, a need to weave the celebration of faith into family life.

To this end, some youth workers have committed themselves to providing mid-week material for families that relates to subjects covered that week at Sunday school. This might be, for example, a handout with illustrations, word searches, key points that can be filled in on a day-to-day basis by parent and child – with different handouts aimed at different age groups.

Alternatively, there are books like *Feast of Faith* by Kevin and Stephanie Parkes, a book that follows the church calendar and festivals such as Lent, Easter, and even Candlemas and Trinity Sunday. It has suggestions for activities, crafts and small dramas that the family can do together during the week. The Parkes wrote the book to help Christian families think through 'what changes can be made that would deepen and define the Christian faith in the home'. In citing James Fowler, a researcher in faith development, they also acknowledge that a household which is passionate about following God displays that passion in the way it prioritizes its time:

> James Fowler defined faith as that which we spend ourselves upon. We 'spend ourselves' on that which is important to us, whether it be football, making money, music, the latest fashion, keeping fit, or our religion.[7]

This isn't just a challenge to parents trying to bring up children in the faith, but a challenge to the entire family of God in Britain living within a deeply secular culture. Celebrating traditions together is one way of resetting our timetables so that faith becomes of paramount importance. When is the family all together? If it's at mealtimes, then that needs to be one point at which faith is discussed, by saying grace, perhaps by reading the Bible together and committing to a family prayer time after the meal is finished.

Again it has to be stressed that if we believe discipleship begins at home, we have to restore parents' confidence in the biblical narrative, and we need to teach them how to engage with tough questions so that they have responses to give to the questions children raise. As Mark Greene, director of LICC, relates, his children are great at coming up with conundrums such as 'If the Koran was written more recently than the Bible, surely it's more reliable?'

In today's world, it seems to me that adult Christians need to be wisdom givers, wisdom sharers and wisdom clarifiers. We must be wisdom givers because there are things our children need to know that we need to tell them. We have to set the agenda in terms of what they should learn about faith. We must be wisdom sharers because our children are used to learning in a way that's interactive. If we don't have the answers to the questions they ask, can we help them find those answers, and by doing so learn ourselves – whether that means going to the internet, to our pastor, or a Bible encyclopaedia? And we must be wisdom clarifiers because they're going to take on board a lot of assumed knowledge about life and the universe over which we have no control, via everything from cartoons, school, magazines and comics to the internet, mobile phones and peers.

'Godly Play'

One great way of encouraging children and their wider families to become more involved in the biblical story is by putting on 'Godly Play' services.

'Godly Play' is an expressive form of telling the Bible story through narrative, symbolism and, of course, play. A narrator starts the story with props – first a box painted gold. One key to the concept of 'Godly Play' is the idea of wondering, so the narrator invites the audience – generally a group of children – to wonder what could be in the box. Because it's gold, children often 'wonder' that something precious must be in there. The narrator will then say that there's a story in the box – it could be a parable – and will explain that stories, particularly Bible stories, are precious. Inside the box are props that help tell the story, so if it's the story of the good shepherd, for example, the narrator will unfold a circle of green felt and invite the children to 'wonder' what it could be – a football pitch, a field, the countryside? The wondering goes on until all the props are out of the box and then the narrator tells the story of the good shepherd using the items at hand.

It's important to understand that 'Godly Play' is not concerned with 'teaching'. Of course, one result of it is that children learn the Bible stories. Another important aspect is that from an early age they're encouraged not just to listen to biblical wisdom, but to interact with it. This reflects a 'rabbinical' approach to learning: think Jesus in the temple at the age of 12, 'wondering' about God and asking big questions. Increasingly, those who work with young people are looking for resources to help them answer big questions about faith. 'Godly Play' is something that helps young people to understand that faith is about asking questions.

Jerome Berryman, a consultant on children's spiritual development, has helped promote 'Godly Play', not because of the importance of teaching, but because of the importance of play. He encourages a holistic view of life, again a diminishing of the sacred/secular divide, and understands that God is interested in play as well as work. He quotes thirteenth-century-thinker St Thomas Aquinas:

> Thomas counselled that Christians need to play and that smiling and laughing are important. He prepared the way

> for the medieval theology of the merry Christian who sees the limits and inadequacy of all created things and for that very reason can move through life with a theological smile.[8]

One church in north-west London has adapted the 'Godly Play' service so that families experience it together. Parents sit with their children and 'wonder' together. After the story the narrator will ask such questions as, 'I wonder which is the most important bit of the story?' Then the parents help their children to do a craft that reflects the parable or Old Testament story. It's a great way for families to begin to see themselves as sacred communities.

4. Be church, be family

Some of the best examples of churches that are reaching out to young people today are not specific youth congregations or youth churches, but churches that aim to be all-age, albeit with a specific remit to reach youth. So they have a strong mission approach to reach young people who've never connected with church before, but they also have a committed adult congregation who aim to make the young people feel as if they belong, opening their homes to them, mentoring them, making them feel like family.

If there's one thing the church should excel at, it's being family, and there are so many ways in which we can do it: worshipping together, learning together, playing together, working together and eating together.

Worshipping together

What do young people want from a worship service? They won't necessarily be expecting bells and whistles, DJs and breakdancers. They may not even be impressed by that approach. What they will note is who's there from their age group and what role they play in the church.

Are young people singing in the choir, handing out communion, doing the Bible reading, creating the Powerpoint slides for the sermon or notices? Do young people preach? If it's only ever adults who perform these tasks, then it sends out clear messages about who has permission to 'speak' – who has permission to take part in these services. John Wimber once said, 'If you want someone to feel involved in church, give them a job to do.' It's true for young and old.

Also, it's vital to allow families to worship together. Make sure you have regular all-age worship services where children don't go out during the service at all, and make sure there's some aspect of every service that's accessible to all ages. The church I attend focuses the first twenty minutes of the service on being all-age, so there are interactive activities like finding people with the same colour hair as you and praying together, children interviewing adults about what they do from Monday to Friday, and vice versa.

Some churches in America are trying radical approaches to ensure that the whole family worships together. Some don't have Sunday school, some don't employ youth workers full stop. Others don't have crèches: why should any parent miss out on teaching because they have to look after their baby elsewhere? You may think that's what God invented PA systems for, but these churches get round it by employing 'baby holders' – volunteers to nurse the baby at the back of the church.

Here's something to think about: if 'family' is the best image we have of church, then can professionalism and perfectionism damage how we do church? If only the best speakers / readers / musicians / technicians are allowed to take part, where's the space for 'apprenticeship' – that is, letting young people just get stuck in? Families often help us grow in confidence because they're places where we're allowed to make mistakes. Too much professionalism can give the impression that mistakes aren't allowed, so who would want to volunteer to be involved up front with such high standards?

Learning together

It's not just young people who love discussing issues raised by teaching. At a recent youth service, my wife Rachel was teaching on relationships. She broke the congregation up into groups for discussion and one couple in particular really appreciated the fact that they got to chat with teenagers about how they had been married for fifty years. Afterwards they insisted that the church should do more services like this.

We can't afford to assume that young people only want to listen to other young people. So if you have youth cells in your church, bring in older people to give their testimony and answer questions. One church in Bournemouth experimented with mixed-age cells – two adults with six young people – and had them meet for consecutive sessions during the sermon time on Sunday mornings. After the end of about six weeks they presented what they'd been learning to the rest of the church.

Similar to this idea is the system employed by some churches of cell twinning. If you have youth cells or young people's house groups in a church, why not twin them with an adult group and have them do joint cells once a month?

Playing together

Make sure that your church does fun events on a regular basis – and not just as outreach. Fish and chips evenings with all-age family quizzes are extremely popular at my church. Churches are slowly waking up to the idea that what's lacking in many areas is community focus, so why not make the church a hub for social events that are family friendly? Whether it's a fun day, a talent evening, a treasure hunt or a mass Monopoly marathon at your church, the focus should be on creating an atmosphere where young and old mingle naturally.

Working together

There's no reason why young and old can't join forces on a whole host of projects – be it building bridges across marshes in Ecuador, repainting the staff room in a local school, setting up fair trade stalls, or being part of the team for holiday clubs. Making sure your church is regularly involved in social action campaigns, local mission or overseas mission trips is one way of ensuring that the whole church family has the opportunity to work out its faith together in a practical way.

Eating together

Many churches have regular monthly meals after the morning service, but I can't underline enough the importance of families practising hospitality in their own homes. The church I attend puts out a sign-up sheet once a month where people can volunteer to be guests or hosts for a meal in someone's home. Often young people go in twos or threes, accompanied by a youth leader, to church members' homes for an evening meal before heading on to church or youth cell. Regular activities like this again help to break down barriers.

5. Prepare children for adulthood, not for adolescence

An important aspect of bridging the gap is also treating our young people as adults before the rest of society does. It's important that we say to our young people as the teen years approach that in God's eyes, in the church's eyes, they're now adults. This means battling against all sorts of social 'conditioning' – patterns of social behaviour that mean every child thinks that rebelling against adult life is the way to express their independence.

A key to treating young people like adults is to let them interact with adults more. I recently led a workshop with a mixed-age range of volunteer and full-time youth workers. Most young people aren't bothered about relevance, but they do want their ideas listened to and respected, so conversation is key to youth work. As Arthur Brown, youth consultant with the Baptist Missionary Society, said in a recent *Youthwork* article:

> People say that youth work and ministry is about teaching. How best do most of us learn? Through talking . . . Sharing ideas with others, allowing the opinions of others to enter our own thought processes. This is especially important for young people as they explore their own identity, values and beliefs.[9]

He goes on to say that most teens do want to be treated as adults and so it matters how we view them. If we see them as children, we'll treat them as such. In their teen years it's important that we afford them the respect we'd afford other adults, even if sometimes they act like children – otherwise how are they going to have their expectations raised? Here's Arthur Brown again:

> Think back to when you were their age. If you are anything like me you wanted the adults around you to treat you as an adult, to talk to you with respect and listen to you and value your opinions – even if those ideas were not fully developed.[10]

Sociologist Tim Edwards echoes this:

> In short, if we expect young people to act like adults, then we need to provide the conditions for them to do so; this involves giving them the same rights and responsibilities that we expect ourselves.[11]

In the workshop we ended up discussing when, where and how we had our best conversations with young people. For a lot of the youth workers the best chats happened during 'extracurricular' activities – in the minibus on the way home from ice skating or after youth group. Also having an excuse to chat to young people works at youth meetings – leading or joining in with a craft, playing cards or board games, or leading a small number in a game like Jenga with forfeits. Some youth workers said that they found out exactly what was happening in the school year, so they knew, for example, when to ask young people how they were doing with their mock GCSEs.

Interaction is one way, but more important is an intentional approach to acknowledging young people's adult status. This can be done through our own 'rites of passage' celebrations and I've mentioned ideas for this elsewhere, but why not also look seriously at what life skills the older people in your church can pass down to the young? It could be anything from orienteering and rock climbing to DIY or first aid. Or why not get someone experienced in business to outline principles for success to the youth group? Getting older people to talk about their careers could really help young people in Year 9, for example, to decide what GCSEs they want to do.

One church from Leeds took a group of young men, all around 15 years old, on a camping trip to the woods with the rest of the blokes from the church. They engaged in several 'skill' activities, including fire making, shelter building and even skinning rabbits! During the day, three different men at different stages of life talked around the fire about their experiences: a middle-aged man talked about being married for thirty years, a first-time father spoke about what it meant to become a parent, and a young man who had recently become engaged chatted about his expectations. It was a truly unforgettable experience for the teenagers, and an amazing rite of passage.

One subtle way of acknowledging children's journey to adulthood is by giving them age-appropriate tasks in the church – increasing responsibility with age. You may not let an 8-year-old loose on the sound desk, but why not let an 11-year-old have a go?

Encouraging maturity isn't simply about what we choose to teach, but about *how* we teach young people. We shouldn't, for example, always presume that some things are for children and some things aren't, such as difficult passages presented in Scripture. As American youth worker Tony Jones notes, a two-dimensional approach to teaching Scripture needs to be avoided:

> Note well, the problem is *not* with scripture – the problem is with foundationalism. In a scientifically oriented world, students are going to ask us, 'how do we really know that the Bible is the word of God?' This is not a question that was asked about the Bible in past centuries – it was a given. Now we try to prove the inerrancy of scripture, and most often we defend it with a self-referential statement: 'because 2 Timothy 3.16 says it is.' That's not proof, it's a circular argument.[12]

We need to broaden our approach if we're going to give young people a substantial comprehension of the authority of Scripture.

Making it work

St Giles's Church in Northampton started the journey towards intergenerational ministry because they wanted to see adults and children brought together and not segregated in 'adult' church and Sunday school. As Pete White, the associate minister, told me, they introduced several aims in order to see change initiated:

1. To develop a new model for congregation meeting that emphasized belonging and relationship.
2. To involve more adults with children, not seeing it as a 'specialist' area of work for those specifically gifted.
3. To encourage those working with children to see themselves as facilitators or group workers rather than teachers – encouraging spiritual growth rather than teaching doctrinal knowledge.
4. To put more resources into equipping parents to 'pass on the faith' at home – through example and home resources/training. Thus to see parents as having primary responsibility for faith formation, not the children's work or church.

All this is framed within a central goal to be 'disciples making disciples' – working towards a narrative approach to the Bible, emphasizing the teaching of the big story of biblical truth and tradition.

In practical terms for them, this means running two services on a Sunday morning – one in the church and one for an intergenerational congregation in the church centre. The intergenerational congregation meets as a whole for worship and Bible story, then splits into age-related small groups which use a 'circle time' model that encourages relationship, sharing and learning together. Adults then have a choice to go and join the other congregation for the sermon or stay for small discussion groups. They then, as Pete says, 'join both congregations together at the end of the morning for prayer, sharing, communion (once a month) etc., oh and the notices of course!'

An important aspect of their work is trying to nurture better relations between young and old by providing more consistent relationships:

> We keep our children in the same groups with same leaders for as long as possible rather than expect them to move groups each year and last year we moved our two Pathfinder groups into the Youth group en bloc with their own leaders coming with them. My hope is that we can thus foster strong peer relationships and relationships with adults who will stay with them through teenage years and by increasing the number of adults involved, we can support parents as extended family might, and also 'normalise' supporting children and even youth work (!) by creating an ethos that sees it as a whole church responsibility to look after our children and young people.

Conclusions

Churches are trying all sorts of experiments with intergenerational ministry – I've mentioned various approaches above. The key to sustaining intergenerational ministry is, as I've suggested, to erode the boundaries that separate 'church' from 'domestic' life.

It's also essential to educate Christian adults so that they can be confident in giving, sharing and clarifying wisdom – so that sharing faith is what happens round the meal table, so that we accept our vocation as 24/7 church, so that we celebrate community. We need to celebrate old age too. Most churches are excellent at reaching out to the elderly in the community, but it's often the case that only thirty-somethings and younger will work with teenagers and only fifty-somethings or older will work with 'twilighters'.

Can we also educate adults so that they no longer 'fear' youth work? We need to recognize that it's a team effort. Our end goal in bridging the generation gap is not to ensure that a few youth workers can build relationships with young people, but to ensure that the entire body of Christ can build such relationships. It's a myth that older people can't do youth work or that they can't relate to youth. Most young people don't expect older people to 'connect' by quoting Dizzee Rascal to them.

The truth is, the better our relationships with our young people before they hit their teens, the better our relationship with them during their teens. This counts for the whole church. This is why we need more interaction across the generations. It's why we need parents to create households that celebrate faith in a way that invites fun, establishes tradition and embraces difficult questions. We need to be wary of the impact of consumerism and our media, we need to raise a generation that can both critique and influence the media, and we need to support our children with extravagant amounts of prayer.

Notes

1. K. C. Dean, *Practising Passion*, p. 25.
2. M. Wroe, *et al.*, *101 Things Jesus Never Said*, p. 70.

3. LICC lecture, 2004.
4. Ibid.
5. M. P. Strommen and R. A. Hardel, *Passing on the Faith*, p. 21.
6. Ibid.
7. K. Parkes and S. Parkes, *Feast of Faith*, p. vii.
8. J. Berryman, *Godly Play*, p. 14.
9. *Youthwork*, May 2006.
10. Ibid.
11. T. Edwards, 'Sexuality', in J. Roche and S. Tucker (eds), *Youth in Society*, p. 174.
12. T. Jones, *Postmodern Youth Ministry*, p. 24.

10. MEND THE GAP

> The Christian mind recognizes that youth's instinct to envelop experiences of music, sex, and communal adventure, with deep, passionate, significance is fundamentally healthy. Youth's tendency to idealize – even to idealize the pop singer and the film star springs from the instinct to spiritualize earthly experience, which is part of redeemed mankind's divine endowment.
> (Harry Blamire, *The Christian Mind*)[1]

Culture bomb

Harry Blamire, writing in the 1960s, recognized that the key to keeping young people engaged with faith was to acknowledge that youthful passion was to be celebrated and nurtured. The faith they embrace should be rooted in authentic worship, but that worship should embrace a diversity of cultural expression. This is true 'whole-life' discipleship: a faith that not only seeks to have something to say about every area of life – be it work or family – but realizes that the range of human experience can be used to glorify God.

The 1960s represented a kaleidoscopic outburst of cultural expression. The world for young people did move from black and white to colour. Unfortunately, the church wasn't equipped to deal with such a culture bomb, as Blamire expands:

> The Christian mind makes sense of passionate youthful longings and dissatisfactions as pointers to the divine creation of man and the fact that he is called to glory. Youth is constitutionally hungry to envelop with religious significance

> the yearnings aroused by natural beauty, by artistic experience, and by sexual love. Because there is no living Christian mind to interpret this hunger and to show how it may be fed, the young are led astray.[2]

It's back to the sacred/secular divide, the church seen as 'good' and the 'world' as bad. You could say that this is due to nearly 2,000 years of 'bad Greek', the church having been influenced by Aristotelian dualism which held that the spiritual world is good while the material world is bad and must be 'escaped'.

When the world came into the living room via full-colour TV, the church had few tools with which to unpack the gamut of new ethical and cultural challenges. Whereas at one time the 'world' could be happily ignored, now we constantly have to reassess what it means to be in the world 24/7 but not of it.

Things have changed, however. Forty years on, parts of the church in the UK recognize that reinvigorating our approach to discipleship – that is, strengthening our ability to engage with the world around us – is essential to unlocking the church's potential to transform the country for Christ. The LICC's 'Imagine' project outlines such an approach. This isn't simply about helping our young people to connect with culture. It's about empowering them to master the culture around them. It's about offering them a robust and passionate faith that says, for example, if pop culture is about creativity then those connected to the Creator should be the best artists out there. But, as Blamire argues, if we're going to feed the spiritual passion of the young, we have to be brimming with that passion ourselves. Every aspect of life, of church, should be shaped by the knowledge that we're 'called to glory'.

Mending the gap is not simply about assessing how we 'plug' young people into adult church. It also means asking whether there's sufficient power supply when we do. Can we feed their faith, their longing? The more I talk to youth workers and church leaders, the more I sense that there's a strong desire within churches to 'mend the gap' – for adults to be reconnected with the young not just as 'service' providers, but as mentors, encouragers and co-workers with Christ. If this is going to happen on a wider scale, then we have to recognize that the task belongs to the wider church body, not just to a handful of individuals.

It takes a village to raise a child

We can't turn back the clock, but we can commit to some much needed repair work to the foundation of community life – the family.

As I discussed earlier, in cultures where the traditional family unit hasn't broken down – that is, outside the Western world – there's less of a problem with the generation gap. It's often only when migrant families move to Western countries that divisions between generations are created.

So it makes sense that establishing a healthy family culture within the church will encourage better relationships between generations. If we separate out 'youth' too much from 'mainstream' adult church, we run the risk of permanently severing communication ties across generations. We end up maintaining the divide, not addressing it.

The following quote from Edwin Friedman, which appears in *Family-Based Youth Ministry* by Mark De Vries, sums up the church's inadvertent mistake in making youth work too much of a separate stream. We thought that the issue could be dealt with in isolation, when in fact the 'problem' of youth culture affects the whole church body:

> When one part of an organism is treated in isolation from its interconnections with another, as though the problem were solely its own, fundamental change is not likely. The symptom is apt to recycle, in the same or different form, in the same or different member. Trying to 'cure' a person in isolation from his or her family . . . is as misdirected, and ultimately ineffective, as transplanting a healthy organ into a body whose imbalanced chemistry will destroy the new one as it did the old. It is easy to forget that the same 'family' or organ that rejects a transplant contributed to the originally diseased part becoming 'foreign'.[3]

You may think this summary overstates the case, but many churches today still believe that simply appointing a youth worker will magically solve all their problems in reaching and keeping young people. We need to recognize that a youth worker alone cannot address the issue. This is an ailment that affects the whole body, and the whole body needs to change. We have to drop the 'overseas mission mentality': how we do youth work is an issue for the whole church to address.

So how do we try to undo the damage? We can start, as this book has done, by repeatedly emphasizing that nurturing children in faith is a corporate responsibility. We shouldn't even think of employing a youth worker unless every adult in the church knows exactly what the church's responsibility is towards young people and is committed to being a part of that process.

A youth worker once told me that he would love to do a survey of how many volunteer youth workers in the church pull out of that ministry as soon as a full-time youth worker is employed. It's a bit like sending reinforcements to your army on the front line and those in the thick of it pulling out and weakening your efforts as soon as replacements arrive. Of course, the reason why many volunteer workers do pull out is that they've been doing it for years with no one to replace them. More people in the church should take on the role in order to spread the load.

The future of intergenerational church

When we consider the future of the church, varying pictures emerge regarding the prospects of mainstream church attracting young people. Many statistics report young people leaving the church in droves, but look at the number of young people with whom church workers have meaningful contact each week. The figure probably reaches into the millions.

So what's the truth? That we're successful at youth mission? That we're successful at reaching young people and putting on outreach events that attract them, but unsuccessful in converting that initial attraction into real church growth?

If that's the case, what's the solution? Do we encourage mono-generational church, church aimed specifically at youth in order to create growth? If we do, we could be in danger of creating a self-fulfilling prophecy. Societal norms in the twenty-first century dictate that the old can't relate to the young and vice versa, so will we always end up trying to separate out our young people into peer groupings in order to keep them interested?

Or is this just a temporary measure? Are we simply waiting for an older generation to die out in the church so that the baton can be handed on to generations who can cope with cultural change? Will the younger generations be the ones who eventually reinvigorate the church with a fresh vision of what it means to be God's kingdom in today's world?

Recently I was asked a common question in youth work today: 'Do you believe that the church can truly bridge the generation gap, or are youth churches inevitable?' It's a big question, but I believe that more and more churches are open to experimenting with traditional church structures. Through the influence of festivals such as Spring Harvest which embrace diverse and creative ways of being church, more and more churches are being encouraged to do things differently. Many churches simply need to find fresh perspectives at leadership level. They need to become experts at listening to younger generations, and inviting younger people into church leadership is one way of accomplishing this.

In light of this, I'm convinced that there are enough resources, stories and fresh perspectives out there to encourage churches to integrate youth work with mainstream congregations. Of course, this can only happen in churches that are open to dynamic change, ones that are prepared to experiment and fail.

Yet there are only so many workers for an increasing number of job postings, and most workers will be attracted to those congregations that already have an existing youth or children's work. You don't need a full-time worker to do intergenerational work, but you do need somewhere to start from, you need a critical mass. Because of this, there are many ageing congregations for whom this type of ministry is simply not a possibility.

When it comes to whether or not youth congregations/churches should exist, then the answer is that they're inevitable. This is a necessity born of mission. As Graham Cray rightly assesses in *Mission-Shaped Youth*, there are such huge numbers of young people who have no link with church at all that we need to begin sowing the seeds of God's kingdom into this generation.[4] The church as it stands won't be able to reach them all.

So many of our youth workers are, effectively, missionaries to an unreached people group – young people who are not just biblically illiterate, but also spiritually illiterate, young people who have struggled at school and who can't get their heads round the language of existing discipleship courses. If we're going to learn how to build a church for the future, we desperately need to support pioneering work that's attempting to reach young people. Someone needs to map this new world so that the rest of us can see where we're going.

If we recognize that our youth workers are missionaries, then we should allow them to do all that's necessary in order to establish God's kingdom in a fresh mission context. That means that if they feel they need to set up 'buffer' churches or youth congregations to sit between outreach work and mainstream Sunday church, then we should allow them to do just that. If they feel they have to set up fresh churches altogether, we should give them our blessing and our financial and prayer support.

A recent idea within the world of business could help us in our thinking about this – the idea of incubation. This involves big businesses allowing small businesses to feed off their resources in order to develop: for instance, a university campus allowing small businesses to use office space at affordable rates.

As churches, therefore, can we 'incubate' youth mission? Can we provide buildings, resources and support to mission-focused youth congregations or churches in order that they grow strong and healthy? And when they can stand on their own two feet, can we have the grace to let them grow independently, while still fostering and mentoring them? There's also an increasing need for adults with a heart for mission to join the ranks of pioneering youth congregations, to open up their homes, to be mentors and 'spiritual' parents. Young Christians need other people apart from youth workers to be role models, otherwise they all end up wanting to be youth workers!

We also need to go further, however. If we do genuinely want youth workers to integrate the young people they reach with mainstream church, then we need to facilitate the necessary changes to make it happen. This means taking on board some of the suggestions in this book and more. But those youth workers need a team behind them. If the church body is not fully behind the integration of young with old, youth work will only ever be a sticking-plaster approach to the problem of the generation gap.

In conclusion

The gospel excels at breaking down traditional social divisions. Youth culture has become one such divide and the church can break it down not through change for change's sake, but through an integral understanding that the church's job is to 'be family'.

This is not an inward-looking or self-serving family, though. It's a family whose focus is on reaching out to the other, to the marginalized, to remove the divides that keep people from being united. The New Testament frequently refers to the idea that our shared love of God is a bond thicker than blood, and so we're to be brothers, sisters and parents to those who are expressly not our kin. As Glenn Miles writes:

> In a culture where the family took precedence over all other relationships, the New Testament church was to reach out to

> the Gentiles, to the unlovely and even to enemies . . . The Christian family is therefore not a safe haven apart from the world, but a powerful witness into the world.[5]

The great unifying power of the cross eroded the barriers set up not only between humankind and God, but between races. In Galatians 3:28 Paul states how radical the work of Christ is, in a culture where Jews would hold funeral services for anyone who married a Gentile in order to symbolize that they were as good as dead.[6] Paul says, 'There is neither Jew nor Greek, slave nor free, male nor female, for you are all one in Christ Jesus.'

It's the passion of the Father, Son and Spirit to see the church grow together as a family. As Stanley Grenz illustrates, at the heart of God is a perfect community, the Trinity, an infinite expression of shared love:

> The God whom Christians proclaim is characterized by love, because this God is triune – the Father, Son and Holy Spirit united in love. Consequently to be the image of God means to reflect the divine love. Because God is this eternal fellowship, we reflect God's character in fellowship with one another.[7]

We express God best when we're united in relationship. That's why Christ says in John 17:23, 'May they be brought to complete unity to let the world know that you sent me and have loved them even as you have loved me.'

That's why we have everything we need to see that work of unity complete: an overwhelming abundance of God's love and spirit. In a society which is only just beginning to realize that the cause of much of its heartache is the breakdown of the family, the church needs to reconnect with the core truth that no one does relational harmony better than the family of God.

To that end, we need to embrace God's vision of young and old *together* making up the complete picture of God's kingdom. As Peter quotes from Joel after the outpouring of the Spirit in Acts 2:17–18:

> In the last days, God says,
> I will pour out my Spirit on all people.
> Your sons and daughters will prophesy,
> your young men will see visions.
> your old men will dream dreams.
> Even on my servants, both men and women,
> I will pour out my Spirit in those days.

It's a beautiful image of how God's Spirit makes no distinction between age or gender. We all have a role in being the voice of God's church. There are many obstacles to overcome in creating a united worshipping family of God, not least the way contemporary secular society has served to diminish the role of elder generations and has often subjected young people to unhelpful social stigma and stereotyping.

For us, though, God is no cultural fable, no mere social construct. Rather he is the constructing force behind society. His ideals for social interaction are the ideals to which we must hold in a rapidly changing world. We're called not simply to be countercultural, but to serve one culture, the greatest story ever told.

Many young people are sold the myth that to be young means to strive for independence or to rebel against adult society. Many Christian young people are told that in a society that denies the validity of their beliefs, they're revolutionaries and countercultural rebels. In fact, we're not the revolution:

we're the authority. A rebel profoundly disagrees with the system of government; we have no objections to Christ's governing of the universe. We're part of his mission to see God's will done on earth as it is in heaven.

I end where I began. Christ's ability to inspire a whole big bad beautiful mix of people to follow him, regardless of their age, has not diminished but burns more brightly and more strongly than it did 2,000 years ago. When men and women truly embrace a passion to see Christ's mission complete, they will find young people compelled also to follow in his footsteps.

Notes

1. H. Blamire, *The Christian Mind*, p. 181.
2. Ibid., p. 180.
3. M. De Vries, *Family-Based Youth Ministry*, p. 58.
4. T. Sudworth, *Mission-Shaped Youth*, pp. 16–19.
5. G. Miles, 'The Development of Children in their Families and Communities', in G. Miles and J. Wright (eds), *Celebrating Children*, p. 36.
6. G. Beynon, *God's New Community*, p. 26.
7. S. Grenz, *What Christians Really Believe and Why*, p. 33.

BIBLIOGRAPHY

Atwater, E. (1988), *Adolescence*, 4th ed., New Jersey: Prentice Hall.

Barham, N. (2006), *Disconnected*, London: Ebury Press.

Beaudoin, T. (2000), *Virtual Faith: The Irreverent Spiritual Quest of Generation X*, New York: Jossey Bass.

Beckwith, I. (2004), *Postmodern Children's Ministry: Ministry to Children in the 21st Century*, Michigan: Zondervan.

Bell, R. (2005), *Velvet Elvis: Repainting the Christian Faith*, Michigan: Zondervan.

Bennett, A. (2001), *Cultures of Popular Music*, Buckingham: Open University Press.

Berryman, J. W. (1995), *Godly Play: An Imaginative Approach to Religious Education*, New York: Augsburg.

Beynon, G. (2005), *God's New Community: New Testament Patterns for Today's Church*, Leicester: IVP.

Blamire, H. (1963), *The Christian Mind*, London: SPCK.

Bradford Brown, B., R. W. Larson and T. S. Saraswathi (eds) (2002), *The World's Youth: Adolescence in Eight Regions around the Globe*, Cambridge: Cambridge University Press.

Brierley, P. (2006), *Pulling Out of the Nosedive: A Contemporary Picture of Churchgoing*, London: Christian Research.

Buckingham, D. (2003), *After the Death of Childhood: Growing Up in the Age of Electronic Media*, Cambridge: Polity Press.

Bunge, M. J. (ed.) (2001), *The Child in Christian Thought*, Michigan: Wm. B. Eerdmans.

Claiborne, S. (2006), *The Irresistible Revolution: Living as an Ordinary Radical*, Michigan: Zondervan.

Cloud, H. and J. Townsend (1992), *Boundaries: When to Say Yes When to Say No to Take Control of Your Life*, Michigan: Zondervan.

Coleman, J. C. and L. B. Hendry (eds) (1999), *The Nature of Adolescence*, 3rd ed., London: Routledge.

Dean, K. C. (2004), *Practising Passion: Youth and the Quest for a Passionate Church*, Michigan: Eerdmans.

De Vries, M. (1994), *Family-Based Youth Ministry*, Illinois: IVP.

Drane, J. (2000), *The McDonaldization of the Church*, London: Darton, Longman & Todd.

Frankel, R. (2001), *The Adolescent Psyche*, Hove: Brunner-Routledge.

Gempf, C. (2003), *Jesus Asked: What He Wanted To Know*, Michigan: Zondervan.

Gerali, S. (2006), *Teenage Guys: Exploring Issues Adolescent Guys Face and Strategies to Help Them*, Michigan: Zondervan.

Gerhardt, S. (2004), *Why Love Matters: How Affection Shapes a Baby's Brain*, Hove: Brunner-Routledge.

Grenz, S. (1998), *What Christians Really Believe and Why*, Louisville: Westminster John Knox Press.

Griffin, C. (1993), *Representations of Youth: The Study of Adolescence and Youth in Britain and America*, Cambridge: Polity Press.

Hebdige, D. (1989), *Subculture: The Meaning of Style*, London: Routledge.

Hilborn, D. and M. Bird (eds) (2002), *God and the Generations: Youth, Age and the Church Today*, Carlisle: Paternoster.

James, A. and A. Prout (eds) (1997), *Constructing and Reconstructing Childhood: Contemporary Issues in the Sociological Study of Childhood*, 2nd ed., London: Falmer Press.

Jensen, A. and L. McKee (eds) (2003), *Children and the Changing Family: Between Transformation and Negotiation*, London: Routledge Falmer.

Jones, T. (2001), *Postmodern Youth Ministry*, Michigan: Zondervan.

Kidner, D. (1971), *Proverbs* (Tyndale Old Testament Commentary), Leicester: IVP.

Kroger, J. (2004), *Identity in Adolescence: The Balance Between Self and Other*, Hove: Routledge.

Lasch, C. (1991), *The Culture of Narcissism: American Life in an Age of Diminishing Expectations*, New York: W.W. Norton & Co.

Lee, N. (2001), *Childhood and Society: Growing Up in an Age of Uncertainty*, Buckingham: Open University Press.

Lesko, N. (2001), *Act Your Age: A Cultural Construction of Adolescence*, New York: Routledge Falmer.

Lyon, D. (2000), *Jesus in Disneyland: Religion in Postmodern Times*, Cambridge: Polity Press.

Mahedi, W. and J. Bernadi (1994), *A Generation Alone: Xers Making A Place in the World*, Illinois: IVP.

Mayo, B., S. Savage and S. Collins (2004), *Ambiguous Evangelism*, London: SPCK.

Miles G. and J. Wright (eds) (2001), *Celebrating Children*, Carlisle: Paternoster.

Mizen, P. (2004), *The Changing State of Youth*, Basingstoke: Palgrave Macmillan.

Morgan, N. (2005), *Blame My Brain: The Amazing Teenage Brain Revealed*, London: Walker Books.

Olson, G. (2006), *Teenage Girls: Exploring Issues Adolescent Girls Face and Strategies to Help Them*, Michigan: Zondervan.

Palmer, S. (2007), *Toxic Childhood: How the Modern World is Damaging Our Children and What We Can Do About It*, London: Orion.

Parkes, K. and S. Parkes (2000), *Feast of Faith: Celebrating the Christian Year at Home*, London: Church House.

Poole, S. (2000), *Trigger Happy: The Inner Life of Videogames*, London: Fourth Estate.

Postman, N. (1985), *Amusing Ourselves to Death: Public Discourse in the Age of Show Business*, New York: Penguin.

Postman, N. (1996), *The Disappearance of Childhood*, London: Vintage Books.

Pountain, D. and D. Robins (2000), *Cool Rules: Anatomy of an Attitude*, London: Reaktion Books.

Quart, A. (2003), *Branded: The Buying and Selling of Teenagers*, London: Arrow.

Roche, J. and S. Tucker (eds) (1999), *Youth in Society*, London: Sage Publications.

Savage, S., S. Collins-Mayo, B. Mayo and G. Cray (2006), *Making Sense of Generation Y: The World View of 15–25 Year Olds*, London: Church House.

Senter, M. H. (gen. ed.) (2001), *Four Views of Youth Ministry*, Michigan: Zondervan.

Sheppard, L. (2002), *Boys Becoming Men: Creating Rites of Passage*, Carlisle: Paternoster.

Sigman, A. (2005), *Remotely Controlled: How Television is Damaging Our Lives*, London: Vermilion.

Sine, T. (1999), *Mustard Seed Versus McWorld: Reinventing Christian Life and Mission for a New Millenium*, London: Monarch.

Strommen, M. P. and R. A. Hardel (2000), *Passing on the Faith: A Radical New Model for Youth and Family Ministry*, Minnesota: St Mary's Press.

Sudworth, T. (2007), *Mission-Shaped Youth*, London: Church House.

Tomlin, G. (2002), *The Provocative Church*, London: SPCK.

Tomlin, G. (2006), *Spiritual Fitness: Christian Character in a Consumer Culture*, London: Continuum.

Udo, T. (2002), *The American Rock Counter Revolution*, London: Sanctuary.

Ward, P. (2005), *Selling Worship: How What We Sing Has Changed the Church*, Milton Keynes: Paternoster.

Winn, M. (2002), *The Plug-In Drug: Television, Computers and Family Life*, London: Penguin.

Withers, M. (2006), *Mission-Shaped Children: Moving Towards a Child-Centred Church*, London: Church House.

Wright, T. (2001), *Luke for Everyone*, London: SPCK.

Wroe, M. (ed.) (1992), *God: What the Critics Say*, Sevenoaks: Hodder & Stoughton.

Wroe, M., A. Reith and S. Parke (1992), *101 Things Jesus Never Said*, London: Marshall Pickering.

APPENDIX 1: GLOSSARY

Definitions of generations

The definitions given below are adapted from *Making Sense of Generation Y*, by Savage, Collins-Mayo, Mayo and Cray, and *God and the Generations*, edited by Hilborn and Bird. For a more developed, near-exhaustive exploration of generational distinctions and differences, see *God and the Generations*. Please note that these are generalizations, and as such paint a broad picture of the make-up of each generation.

Builder Generation

Born between 1925 and 1945. A relatively conservative generation who both protected and built on their parents' achievements – 'building' a future after World War II. This generation experienced the post-war reverberations that would give birth to youth culture, largely a post-war consumerist boom that meant young people had disposable income for the first time. Advertisers and marketers identified this group as 'teenagers'. This type of targeted marketing meant there was a growing tension between the wants of teenagers and the wants of their parents. The result was a friction between conservatism and self-expression.

Boomer Generation

Born between 1946 and 1963, and so called because of the increase in the birth rate after World War II. If the Builders dipped their toes in the sea of 'youth culture' and teen rebellion, then Boomers – in more ways than one – started surfing it. They were the children of the 1960s whose values were radically different from those of their parents. They espoused largely liberal progressive ideals and looked forward to a world that enjoyed material prosperity without the social and moral constraints imposed upon it by previous generations.

Matures

'Matures' is a generic term that refers to people over the age of 50 – a mix of 'Boomers' and 'Builders'. Within the context of this book, it refers to a mix of church stalwarts and pioneers who, through the mere fact of their age and generational leanings, have either a limited comprehension of the needs of burgeoning generations or, if they perceive them, often a reluctance to adapt in order to meet those needs.

Generation X (Gen X, Xers)

Born between 1964 and 1981. Also referred to as the **Buster Generation**, as there was a dip in the birth rate after the population spurt of the Boomers. Gen X had many reasons to challenge the progressive optimism of previous generations. They saw huge rises in divorce rates as well as economic recessions and the spread of AIDS. Although the generational name was used in a study of British youth in the 1960s, it was popularized by an eponymous punk band fronted by Billy Idol, but more famously it was the title of a book by Canadian author Douglas Coupland – *Generation X: Tales for an Accelerated Culture*. His book painted a picture of a generation disenchanted with all the many changes forced upon it and in particular the obsessions of capitalist success and excess, money, career and status.

Generation Y (Gen Y)

Also known as the **Millennial Generation** or the **Internet Generation**. Born from 1982 onwards. This is the grouping most affected by the rapid advance of information and communication technology and heightened consumerism. It's a generation adept at multi-tasking, focused on pleasure seeking and at once overtly aware of but beholden to the pressures society places on it. So while members of Gen Y are aware of the heightened ability for self-expression, they're also aware of the need to conform in order to fit in.

APPENDIX 2: RESOURCES

The following is a list of resources – reading, websites and courses – connected to the five principles for creating integrated church which were outlined in chapter 9.

1. Restore confidence in our ability to pass down the faith

Reading

S. Grenz, *What Christians Really Believe and Why*, Westminster John Knox Press. A great introduction to faith for non-believers and insightful conversational apologetics for believers.

A. Orr-Ewing, *Why Trust the Bible? Answers to Ten Relevant Questions*, IVP. Thorough and compelling analysis of the reliability of the Bible. Insist that your church gets a teaching series on this book.

R. Briggs, *Light to Live By: How to Interpret the Bible*, Scripture Union. Accessible and enlightening approach to engaging with Scripture.

Courses

Toolbox: A five-day training course designed to help Christians respond to the challenges of living in today's world. For leaders and laity. See www.licc.org.uk/toolbox.

Foundations 21: An online discipleship course tailored to different learning styles which provides a wealth of resources for churches, small groups and individuals. See www.foundations21.com.

Small group studies

Imagine: A one-session DVD introduction to whole-life discipleship from the LICC. See http://www.licc.org.uk/imagine/dvd.

Glad You Asked: A 10-session DVD aimed at introducing the faith to the 'spiritually curious', but again a great conversational apologetics overview for Christians. See www.gladyouasked.org.

Christian Life and . . . : Various topics covered, from biblical interpretation to contemporary apologetics, in a series of DVD studies from The London School of Theology. See www.christianlifeand.com.

2. Emphasize the role of family as sacred community

Reading

M. P. Strommen and R. A. Hardel, *Passing on the Faith*, St Mary's Press. As well as presenting an in-depth model on how to encourage youth and family ministry, there are many practical suggestions for how families can nurture a culture of discipleship within the home.

G. Miles and J. Wright (eds), *Celebrating Children*, Paternoster. In-depth material on the representation of children and families within the Bible.

I. Beckwith, *Postmodern Children's Ministry*, Zondervan. See in particular chapter 6 on 'Family Matters', looking at the spiritual responsibilities of the family unit.

Practical

Parkes, K. and S. Parkes, *Feast of Faith*, Church House. Practical suggestions for parents that connect with the church calendar; includes prayers, crafts, readings and decorations.

Faith at Home: A website that offers a huge amount of resources and activities to help you nurture children's spirituality, including advice on how to do 'Godly Play' at home. See www.faith-at-home.com.

3. Train parents

Most of the suggestions for points 1 and 2 connect with equipping parents to be better disciples and helping them to pass on the faith, but helping them simply to be better parents is obviously key to assisting them in modelling faith to their children. The following are suggestions for helping adults to develop parenting skills.

Reading

S. Gerhardt, *Why Love Matters*, Brunner-Routledge. Gerhardt focuses on why love and affection are so vital in the early years of a child's development.

N. Morgan, *Blame my Brain*, Walker Books. Interesting insight into the development of the brain during adolescence and how it influences teenagers' behaviour.

N. Pollard, *Teenagers: Why Do They Do That?*, Damaris Publishing. This doesn't just provide an analysis of teen behaviour, but also offers constructive advice for communicating with young people.

S. Palmer, *Toxic Childhood: How the Modern World is Damaging Our Children and What We Can Do About It*, Orion. The title pretty much says it all. Get parents in your church to read it and ask them if they agree with Palmer's findings.

Small group studies

The Parent Talk Parenting Course: Video-led sessions by Rob Parsons. The Parent Talk website features a cornucopia of resources and information on parenting. See www.parenttalk.co.uk.

Practical

Care for the Family provide online support for parents facing any issue connected with raising a family. See www.careforthefamily.org.uk/supportnet.

4. Be church, be family

Reading

M. De Vries, *Family-Based Youth Ministry*, IVP. A great discussion of why family work is essential to youth ministry, and a practical manual on how to develop a family focus within church.

M. H. Senter (gen. ed.), *Four Views of Youth Ministry*, Zondervan. The first view deals with integrating young people into congregations, the second with preparing youth for leadership and life in adult church, the third looks at the whole area of youth ministry as mission, and the fourth deals with the feasibility of youth congregations.

M. Withers, *Mission-Shaped Children*, Church House. Provides case studies of how churches across the UK are developing cutting-edge children's work, as well as suggestions for working towards integrated all-age church.

J. Berryman, *Godly Play*, Augsburg. An inventive approach which balances reverence for the biblical narrative with engaging storytelling. Details of training can be found at www.godlyplay.org.uk.

Practical
All Age Service Annual: Scripture Union have recently redeveloped their resources for all-age services. See http://www.scriptureunion.org.uk/light/lightyearstaster.asp.

5. Prepare children for adulthood, not for adolescence

Reading
T. Sudworth, *Mission-Shaped Youth*, Church House. Essential reading as it asks many questions about integrating youth and church and provides cutting-edge examples of ministry with young people.

S. Gerali, *Teenage Guys: Exploring Issues Adolescent Guys Face and Strategies to Help Them*, Zondervan. A guidebook for helping young men navigate adolescence.

G. Olson. *Teenage Girls: Exploring Issues Adolescent Girls Face and Strategies to Help Them*, Zondervan. Guess!

D. E. Green and M. Green, *Taking a Part: Young People's Participation in Church*, Church House. Focuses on how to bring marginalized youth into the centre of church life.

H. Cloud and J. Townsend, *Boundaries*, Zondervan. Comes across a little too much like a self-help manual, but nevertheless an important discussion of how to set boundaries. If we're trying to help young people mature, we need to help them establish boundaries for themselves.

M. Paver, *Wolf Brother*, Orion. An excellent fantasy novel set 6,000 years ago. The hero, Torak, is taught everything he needs in order to survive by his father. Great for reflecting on the relationship between adults and children.

Practical
Dads'n'Lads Weekend: Lee Abbey have started putting on activity weekends for parents and offspring. An invaluable bonding experience which could be used as a rite of passage. See www.leeabbey.org.uk.

Essential: The Evangelical Alliance's project for providing youth workers with vital resources for discipling young people. Lots of answers to difficult questions, ideas for training, and reviews of available books, small group studies, etc. Really worth looking at regularly.
See www.essential-truth.org.